FOLLOW-UP EVANG

FOLLOW UP EVANGELISM

W. Hal Brooks

BROADMAN PRESS

Nashville, Tennessee

ISBN: 0–8054–2519–5
Dewey Decimal Classification: 268.43
Printed in the United States of America

To the North Richland Hills Baptist Church, Fort Worth, Texas, where it has been my privilege to pastor for thirteen years, and to the many faithful members who patiently labored with me to put into practice the principles of follow-up evangelism.

FOREWORD

Those who have studied the church located in the suburbs have made some rather frightening accusations. One of these is that the church in the suburbs does not so much convert the community as it baptizes it. One of the great problems in the church is not so much that of reaching people for church membership, but the problem of leading them into a vital, growing relationship to Christ and a meaningful church relationship.

W. Hal Brooks is pastor of a church in the fastest growing area of a city. He has been made aware not only of the need to enlist people but also of the continuing responsibility in the spiritual development of Christians. This book is the result of that concern.

The author has drawn from a number of sources. His desire is to bring together those materials and approaches which will most benefit any size church in helping the new convert or the new church member. This book is his first step in publication. It deserves careful attention for several reasons:

First, he is not writing from the slightly more remote position of seminary professor or evangelism secretary. He is writing in the context of a local church where he works day by day.

Second, this is not a program which is presented as an easy cureall for the problems of a church in similar situations. Everything recommended takes work. That which meets the needs in one church at one time does not always meet the needs in all churches at all times, therefore, the approach has been designed to be flexible.

Third, before this book was written, he took the basic ideas and materials in the book and used them in a spiritual development program in his church. Others have since used the program. The results were highly successful.

One of the most exciting areas relating to evangelism in this decade is the renewed interest in spiritual development as a part of evangelism. It will be a wonderful day for evangelism when everyone realizes that there is more involved than confronting a person with the gospel and seeking an initial response. I'm thankful for the author and his church and his efforts in this book as it points us in that direction.

KENNETH L. CHAFIN
Director, Division of Evangelism,
Home Mission Board,
Southern Baptist Convention

PREFACE

What pastor has not faced the discouraging realization that the largest percentage of his church membership is inactive and indifferent? Every pastor has felt the heartache caused by those who profess Christ and yet never grow in Christian character; never become involved in Christian service; never experience victory over life's temptations.

Church "drop-outs" are a constant source of concern and embarrassment to most churches and their leadership. If we really care, we must ask ourselves, "Why?" What happens to so many who never get involved in the fellowship of a church?

An easy answer is that these people have never been genuinely saved; and in many cases this may be true. But this answer is neither honest nor adequate, for there are multitudes who have been converted, yet still they are inactive, ineffective, defeated Christians. Again, if we are honestly concerned, we must ask, "Why?"

It would be presumptuous for any one person to give a simple answer to this complex problem. However, most Christian leaders who have studied the problem feel that the churches have not been successful in properly guiding and training young believers into a full Christian experience.

Educational institutions of America have become vitally concerned about the school drop-outs. Millions of dollars yearly are spent coping with this problem. Yet, it is a sad fact that most churches accept the spiritual drop-outs as "normal business." We spend very little time or money dealing with one of our greatest problems.

For a pastor or layman who is willing to discover the simple principles of person-to-person ministry this vast army of indifferent members will be a great challenge rather than a discouragement. One of the greatest needs of our day is for a program of total New Testament evangelism, a FOLLOW-UP EVANGELISM, in every church.

This book is an attempt to share the basic principles of total New Testament evangelism with particular emphasis upon follow-up. It is the author's prayer that the thoughts contained in these materials will be only a springboard for pastors and laymen to launch into even greater programs for "feeding the lambs and caring for the sheep." May I suggest the following?

PROGRAM PROCEDURE

1. *Study the principles and programs as outlined in this book.*
2. *Train all Sunday School workers and deacons using this book as a study guide.*
   (1) The training of the initial workers should be done by the pastor. However, the basic principles must be continuously stressed to the Sunday School workers and deacons. The initial training may be done during a one week period such as the Sunday School preparation week. Some churches have made it a part of their church training program on Sunday evenings. Still others have conducted training prior to a revival; they began using the decision counselors in the revival services.
   (2) Out of the groups of trained workers, some should be selected to serve as decision counselors. Many churches have trained the deacons and their wives for this special task. It has been found that from ten to twenty counselors are needed for an average size church. There should be an equal number of men and women.
3. *Select a Director of Follow-Up.* He should be a layman who has a vision for this work and will give leadership to the work. As Paul said, he should be ". . . a faithful man" (1 Tim. 2:2). He will be responsible for preparing the counseling room, keeping check on the workers needs, checking on the visitation results, and assisting in any way possible.
4. *Prepare or secure the necessary materials:*
   (1) A Decision Card. Printed decision cards are available from Baptist Book stores.
   (2) An Initial Visit Card. This card will need to be mimeographed or printed. This card is to be given or mailed to the Sunday School

teacher to use in making an initial home visit. A sample of this card is given in this book.

(3) Sunday School Individual Record Card. The basic Sunday School class attendance record card is all that is needed to keep check on the progress of the new member. If a new Christian is continuously absent, or does not study his Bible, this reveals a very real need for help. It is suggested that a rubber stamp could be made with the following: "NEW CHURCH MEMBER—(Needs Special Care)." This could be stamped with red ink somewhere on the record card. This would remind the teacher that this person is a new church member and needs extra special care.

(4) Bible study materials. A special booklet, "YOUR LIFE IN CHRIST" has been prepared to be used as a beginning Bible study for new members and new Christians. It is available from Baptist Book Stores.

W. HAL BROOKS

CONTENTS

CONTENTS

FOLLOW-UP EVANGELISM

PART ONE

PRINCIPLES OF
FOLLOW-UP
EVANGELISM

Chapter 1

WHAT IS
FOLLOW-UP
EVANGELISM?

"Follow-Up Evangelism" is a phrase not found in the New Testament. However, the basic concepts and principles are interwoven throughout. It is an evangelism which follows through—and a follow-through which produces evangelism. It is spiritual life producing spiritual life. Follow-up evangelism is the work of a local church in protecting, training, and guiding a "babe in Christ" in order that he may develop into a growing, useful, victorious Christian in every area of life.

A local congregation of Christian believers in God's unique strategy for reaching a man from birth to death. No other organization on the earth seeks to meet the spiritual needs of a man for his whole lifetime. Some groups attempt to meet needs at various levels of a person's life, such as high school or college. But only the local church seeks to deal with a man for life. Follow-up evangelism is concerned about the Christian's full life.

God's purpose for the local church is to unite Christians as a spiritual family. Church members are to build up, not tear down one another. God has placed men in families for their care, protection, fellowship, companionship, and development. If a family is weak, you do not destroy it, you try to strengthen it. A church exists for the purpose of meeting the spiritual needs of the children of God. If the local church is weak and ineffective, simply criticizing it or its leadership is not the answer. It must be strengthened, not destroyed.

Paul warned the Christians at Rome, "I appeal to you, brethren,

21

to be on your guard concerning those who create dissensions and difficulties and cause divisions, in opposition to the doctrine—the teaching—which you have been taught. (I warn you to turn aside from them, to) avoid them. For such persons do not serve our Lord Christ but their own appetites, and base desires, and by ingratiating and flattering speech they beguile the hearts of the unsuspecting and simple-minded (people)" (Rom. 16:17,18).

We need the church for all the reasons we need a family and many more. Care, love, protection, instruction, fellowship and companionship are all essential ingredients of a strong family, or a good church.

A careful study of Christ's commission will reveal the basic mission of every church: "Go then and make disciples of all the nations, baptizing them into the name of the Father and of the Son and of the Holy Spirit, teaching them to observe everything that I have commanded you, and lo, I am with you all the days—perpetually, uniformly, and on every occasion—to the very close and consummation of the age" (Matthew 28:19–20).

In this passage the mission of the church is clearly defined as a twofold task: (1) *Witnessing* to the lost, (2) and *teaching* and *training* the saved. It is often thought that the imperative command of the Great Commission is found in the word "go," verse 19. However, this word is a *past participle,* more accurately translated, "having gone," or "as you go." It seems that Jesus was assured His disciples would go into the world, and the reason was because of the actual imperative command of the commission. This is found in the word "teach," verse 19, more accurately translated, "make disciples." In verse 20, the word "teach" is a different word from that in verse 19.

The word in verse 20 is a *present participle* meaning to build up, to bring to maturity. It means to spiritually equip the new Christian with the TRUTH of Jesus Christ. It was not to be a one time event, but a continuing process. In this Jesus revealed how a believer is to be brought to maturity. He was saying, "As I have taught you how to live, now you must continously teach others how to live." Teaching and training the disciples how to live was of primary importance to the Lord Jesus. How important is it to us?

New Testament evangelism's total objective is not only to see the sinner converted, but also to see him growing into a victorious, useful Christian. One aspect cannot be neglected at the expense of the other. Follow-up evangelism is the carrying out of this total commission of Christ to the Church. It is primarily and basically to be done through the work of the local church. This is the work of every Bible teaching Sunday School worker. This is the work of every deacon. This is the work of the pastor. It is to be the work of every believer.

In Acts 2:41–42 we find a specific picture of this total concept of evangelism being carried out. "Then those who received His word with approval were immersed. And there were added to their number on that day about three thousand souls. And they were giving constant attention to the teaching of the apostles doctrine and to that which they held in common with them, and to the breaking of the bread and to the gatherings where prayers to God were offered."— (Wuest Translation.) These young believers were continuously taught the truth of Christ as they met together in spiritual fellowship and prayer.

According to the New Testament, *it is as sinful not to teach and train new converts as it is not to baptize them.*

A vivid picture of this New Testament concept of Follow-up evangelism can be seen in Paul's conversion and all that follows. Evidence seems to reveal that Paul was converted on the road to Damascus. He cried out, "Who are you, Lord?" and "What will you have me do?" In these two questions are involved the issues of life, the discovery of Jesus Christ as a person, and the discovery of His purpose of life.

Christ revealed Himself uniquely to Paul on that road. Yet, the Lord used a devout man, Ananias, to teach Paul "what he must do." Paul needed follow-up. When Ananias met Paul, he spoke to him as "Brother Saul" seeming to indicate that Paul's conversion had already taken place. Now he needed instruction. Ananias proceeded to instruct him about a new purpose of life. "And he said, the God of our forefathers has destined and appointed you to come progressively to know His will—that is, to perceive, to recognize more strongly and clearly and to become better and more intimately acquainted with His will; and to see the Righteous One Jesus Christ, the Messiah and to hear a voice from His (own) mouth and a message from His (own) lips; For you will be His witness unto all men of everything that you have seen and heard" (Acts 22:14–15). Paul was *taught* the will of God and *trained* to be a witness of the Lord.

Whether the conversion experience be as dramatic as Paul's or as simple as a child's the follow-up need is the same; to be *taught* the will of God and be *trained* to be His witness unto all men.

THIS WORK MUST BE A PERSON-TO-PERSON MINISTRY

It is not so much a program as it is a person; not simply materials furnishing facts, but men sharing lives. It is a mind to mind, heart to heart, man to man ministry in building up the lives of new or immature believers.

A classic example of the importance of the personal touch can be seen in the story of the raising of Lazarus from the dead. Jesus called for Lazarus to come forth out of the grave. But he asked men to roll back the stone. God's method is men. Lazarus was given resurrection life, but he was still bound with the grave clothing. Jesus had called him forth from the grave and had given him life, but he asked others to free him of the grave clothing.

When someone accepts Christ as Lord and Savior, he is given resurrection life, but he still can be bound with old habits and temptations. Our Lord has given us the responsibility of teaching and training young believers with the Word of God in order that each may grow up into maturity.

(1) FOLLOW-UP EVANGELISM INVOLVES RESPONSIBLE CONCERN

Jesus said to Peter, "Simon, son of John, do you love me—with a deep, instinctive, personal affection for Me, as for a close friend? Peter was grieved—took it ill—that He should ask him the third time, Do you love Me? And he said to Him, Lord, you know everything; you know that I love you—that I have a deep, instinctive, personal affection for You, as for a close friend. Jesus said to him, "Feed My sheep" (John 21:17).

Paul had such deep concern for the Christians in Thessalonica that he wrote: "(And we) continue to pray especially and with most intense earnestness night and day that we may see you face to face and mend and make good whatever may be imperfect and lacking in your faith" (1 Thess. 3:10). He was so concerned that he felt he would die if they didn't stand firm in the Lord (1 Thess. 3:8).

To the Romans Paul wrote: "For I am yearning to see you, that I may impart and share with you some spiritual gift to strengthen and establish you" (Romans 1:11). Paul was so sensitive and aware of his responsibility that he said, "But we behaved gently when we were among you, like a devoted mother nourishing and cherishing her own children" (1 Thess. 2:7).

He felt that total evangelism was like spiritual parenthood. We have a responsibility to these "babes in Christ" to love, feed, protect, and train them in their walk in Christ. Paul taught, "Brethren, if any person is overtaken in misconduct or sin of any sort, you who are spiritual—who are responsive to and controlled by the Spirit—should set him right and restore and reinstate him, without any sense of superiority and with all gentleness, keeping an attentive eye on your-self, lest you should be tempted also. Bear (endure, carry) one an-other's burdens and troublesome moral faults, and in this way fulfill and observe perfectly the law of Christ, the Messiah, and complete what is lacking in (your obedience to it)" (Gal. 6:12).

A baby is not responsible to his parents until he grows a bit older, but from the beginning the parents are responsible to the baby. Parents are to love their children, feed them, protect them, and train them. These are the same responsibilities we have to every immature believer, to every young convert.

Paul wrote to the Thessalonians: "For you know how, like a father (dealing with) his children, we used to exhort each of you personally, stimulating and encouraging and charging you to live lives worthy of God" (1 Thess. 2:11–12).

And to the Corinthians he wrote: "I do not write this to shame you, but to warn and counsel you as my beloved children. After all, though you should have ten thousand teachers (guides to direct you) in Christ, yet you do not have many fathers. For I became your father in Christ Jesus through the glad tidings (the Gospel)" (1 Cor. 4: 14–16).

(2) FOLLOW-UP EVANGELISM MUST INVOLVE PERSONAL CONTACT

Although Paul wrote many letters to young converts and also prayed for them, he considered *PERSONAL CONTACT* and *TIME WITH THEM* to be most essential to effectively build up their lives in Christ. A Bible teacher who will not make personal contacts with those he is endeavoring to teach will not meet their needs.

When Paul had preached the gospel in the cities of Asia Minor, he returned to his home church and then, ". . . after some time Paul said to Barnabas, come, let us *go back and again visit, and help, and minister* to the brethren in every town where we made known the message of the Lord, and SEE HOW THEY ARE GETTING ALONG" (Acts 15:36).

Of the Thessalonians he prayed night and day that he might see them face to face to mend whatever was lacking in their faith (1 Thess. 3:10).

To the Romans Paul wrote: "For I am yearning to see you" (Rom. 1:11). Personal contact is a vital key to proper teaching and training of new Christians.

FOLLOW-UP EVANGELISM HAS AN OVERALL THREEFOLD OBJECTIVE

(1). The first objective is to teach the new Christian *how to walk* a normal victorious life *in Christ*.

"But I say, walk and live habitually in the (Holy) Spirit—responsive to and controlled and guided by the Spirit; then you will certainly not gratify the cravings and desires of the flesh—of human nature without God" (Gal. 5:16).

The Christian life is more than a step. It is described as a walk. Many have taken the first step of faith, the acceptance of Jesus Christ into their lives, but they have not continued to walk daily in Him. They are saved, but stuck. To be born of the Spirit is only the beginning of the Christian life. Then should follow a lifetime in which the believer is to develop spiritual maturity. He is to grow up and go on. But what is growth? Spiritual growth has to do with spiritual knowledge.

Jesus commanded the apostles to teach others to live as He had taught them how to live (Matt. 28:19–20). Paul could say of the Christians with whom he had worked, "You learned from us about how you ought to walk so as to please and gratify God, as indeed you are doing; that you do so attaining yet greater perfection in living this life (1 Thess. 4:1).

Pleasing God is the purpose of the Christian's life. How do we please God? By faith! "Without faith," Paul said, "it is impossible to please God" (Heb. 11:6). What is faith and how do we get faith? Faith is basically trusting God. It is dependence upon God. It comes from learning truth. "So faith comes by hearing (what is told) and what is heard comes by preaching (of the message that came from the lips) of Christ" (Rom. 10:17). For us not to teach *every* new Christian the truth *as it is in Jesus* is as criminal as not feeding new born infants.

God has given gifted men to the church for the specific purpose of teaching the immature Christian how to walk in Christ. "And His gifts were (varied; He Himself appointed and gave men to us) some to be apostles (special messengers), some prophets (inspired preachers and expounders), some evangelists (preachers of the Gospel, traveling missionaries), some pastors (shepherds of His flock), and teachers. *His intention was the perfecting and the full equipping of the saints* (His consecrated people), (that they should do) the work of ministering toward building up Christ's body (the church), (that it might develop until we all attain oneness in the faith and in the comprehension of the full and accurate knowledge of the Son of God; that (we might arrive) at really mature manhood—the completeness of personality which is nothing less than the standard height of Christ's own perfection—the measure of the stature of the fullness of the Christ, and the completeness found in Him. *So then, we may no longer be children, tossed (like ships) to and fro between chance gusts of teaching, and wavering with every changing wind of doctrine. . . ."* (Eph. 4:11–14).

As the new Christian grows in his knowledge of the Lord Jesus, he learns how to walk in a manner fully pleasing to the Lord. Paul continuously prayed for the young Christians at Colassae. "We . . . have not ceased to pray and make (special) requests for you, (Asking) that you may be filled with the full (deep and clear) knowledge of His will in all spiritual wisdom (that is, in comprehensive insight into the ways and purposes of God) and in understanding and discernment of spiritual things; that you may walk (live and conduct yourselves) in a manner worthy of the Lord, fully pleasing to Him and desiring to please Him in all things, bearing fruit in every good work and steadily growing and increasing in (and by) the knowledge of God" (Col. 1:9,10).

(2). A second aspect of the total objective is to guide the Christian growing in a knowledge of the Lord Jesus to become a faithful *WITNESS* to share with others his experience in Christ.

Jesus' very last word to His disciples while on this earth was that they should be His witnesses to the very ends of the earth (Acts 1:8). John said, "What we have seen and (ourselves) heard we are also telling you. . . ." (1 John 1:3) Ananias instructed Paul: "For you will be His witness unto all men of everything that you have seen and heard" (Acts 22:15).

If a man is properly discipled or taught, the natural result of his life will be to *GO* and *WITNESS,* sharing his experiences in Christ with others. If a man is walking in Jesus, he will naturally witness. If he doesn't witness, there is something wrong with his walk.

Jesus said in Matthew 4:19, "Follow me, and I will make you fishers of men." His command is to follow Him: the promise is that as we do, He will make us to become fishers of men. It is the following that makes us fishers of men.

It is, therefore, essential that we teach a young Christian how to walk in Christ in order that he might effectively witness of his experiences in Christ.

Jesus told a young man, "Go home to your own (family and relatives and friends), and bring back word to them of how much the Lord has done for you, and (how He has) and sympathy for you and mercy on you" (Mark 5:19).

A third aspect of the total objective of follow-up evangelism is to train each Christian to follow up or work with any new convert or immature Christian whom God may entrust to his care. This completes the cycle of total New Testament evangelism. "And the (instructions) which you have heard from me, along with many witnesses, transmit and entrust (as a deposit) to reliable and faithful men who will be competent and qualified to teach others also" (2 Tim. 2:2).

Someone taught Paul. He taught Timothy. Timothy was to teach reliable and faithful men. The faithful men were to teach others. Thus is pictured the full cycle of total evangelism: walking in Christ—witnessing to the lost—working with the new convert, teaching him to walk in Christ, to witness to the lost, to work with new converts.

Chapter 2

WHY DO
FOLLOW-UP
WORK?

There are two basic essentials in successful Christian work: One is direction and the second, is motivation. Of the two, motivation is the most difficult. A church must know where it is going before it can get there. But it may know *what* to do and *never* do it. The secret of a church being successful in doing follow-up work will be understanding what to do and why it must be done.

Paul said, "Whatever you may do, do all for the honor and glory of God" (1 Cor. 10:31). Is it possible that we have lost some of the true motives of our evangelistic work. Our work must bring glory and honor to Christ Jesus (Eph. 3:21). It could be that we have allowed some of the highly competitive spirit of the world to influence our motives in the work of Christianity. Do we do our work for the praise of man or the glory of God? What would happen if we were to publish our evangelistic results, not on the number of converts won during revivals or witnessing emphases, but on the number who are faithful and growing in spiritual knowledge after just ONE FULL YEAR? This is not suggested, but it does illustrate that we often work the hardest for that for which we get the most acclaim.

1. *A basic motivation for our doing follow-up work is a desire to fully obey Christ.* Has Christ commanded us to "feed the lambs and the sheep?" Has He exhorted us to teach and train believers about how to live? If we are to be fully obedient to Christ's commands, we cannot neglect to follow up those who are entrusted to our care. Follow-up work is an essential part of the Great Commission. It is as vital as

witnessing to the lost. Samuel reminded King Saul, "Behold, to obey is better than sacrifice" (1 Samuel 15:22). Most feel it is a great sin to neglect to witness to the lost. Yet, it is as equally sinful not to teach and train new Christians.

2. *Another basic motivation is love.*

(1) First is our love of Christ. This is the strongest single motivation for our doing follow-up work. If we have a genuine love for Christ, we will have a desire to care for each precious young believer whom He loves. "When they had eaten, Jesus said to Simon Peter, Simon, Son of John, do you love me . . .? He said to Him, Yes, Lord; You know that I love you—that I have deep instinctive personal affection for you, as for a close friend. He said to him *feed my lambs* . . . My sheep" (John 21:15,16,17).

(2) Second is our love for the new Christian. "And may the Lord make you to increase and excel and overflow in love for one another and for all people, just as we also do for you. So that He may strengthen and confirm and establish your hearts faultlessly pure and unblamable in holiness in the sight of our God and Father, at the coming of our Lord Jesus Christ, the Messiah, with all His saints—the Holy and glorified people of God! Amen, so be it." (1 Thess. 3:12,13). Jesus said, "By this shall all (men) know that you are my disciples, if you love one another—if you keep on showing love among yourselves" (John 13:35). The greatest single characteristic of the first New Testament church was its love among the membership. Paul wrote to the church at Thessalonica, "So, being this tenderly and affectionately desirous of you, we continued to share with you not only God's good news (the Gospel) but also our own lives as well, for you had become so very dear to us" (1 Thess. 2:8).

3. Still another *MOTIVE is WORLD EVANGELIZATION.* If we genuinely desire to reach the whole world with the Gospel, it is absolutely essential that we care for each new convert. Jesus has given us our generation as our responsibility . . . "and you shall be My witnesses in Jerusalem and all Judea and Samaria and to the ends— the very bounds—of the earth" (Acts 1:8). He promised that before He returned to the earth, the gospel will have been preached in all the world (Matthew 24:14). Surely, there is no greater motivation for

getting the Gospel out to the whole world than to hasten the coming of our Lord Jesus.

(1) Follow-up evangelism is the *quickest way* to witness to the whole world. If one witnesses to one, and both witness to another, and this continues with converts being won by every Christian every six months: at the end of sixteen years, if no one should fail, there would be over three billion converts won to Christ. Of course, this is only a theory, but it does point out that it is actually possible to witness to the world in our generation as Christ commanded.

(2) Follow-up evangelism is the *only way* to win the world. No one person could possibly witness to the world in his lifetime. If he could witness to ten per day, it would take well over two million years just to witness to the population. It is, therefore, only reasonable that he must have help. This help must come from his converts and their converts. It was said in the book of Acts that the disciples multiplied and the Lord added to His church. Charles H. Spurgeon once said, "He who converts a soul draws water from a fountain; but he who trains a soul-winner digs a well from which thousands may drink to eternal life." Following up each new Christian is imperative and essential if we are to *see the world* come to know Christ in our time.

NOT ALL WILL RESPOND

It is important to realize that not everyone will respond. A broken-hearted Saviour once said to some unfaithful followers. "Why call ye me Lord, Lord and do not the things I say?" (Luke 6:46). Paul once said, "Demas hath forsaken me, having loved this present world too much" (2 Timothy 4:10). It is not our responsibility that they respond, but it is our responsibility to teach them how they should respond.

Some genuine believers will respond more slowly than others. After Jesus worked almost three years with Peter, he still denied the Lord three times. In his second epistle, Peter reveals that his basic problem was that he had not fully realized all of the truth about the Lord Jesus. At first, he thought Christianity was what he could do for God and he failed miserably. Then he discovered that Christianity is what God can do for a man and he lived in the joy of victory. Peter shared that some of these things are hard to understand, and those who are

unlearned will be unstable and finally defeated (2 Peter 3:16). Therefore, he warned all Christians to "grow in grace, and in the knowledge
of our Lord and Saviour Jesus Christ" (2 Peter 3:18).

There will be those who have never been born again scattered
among the believers. These, of course, cannot grow spiritually because
they have never actually become children of God. Jesus chose the
twelve and one of them turned out to be a devil. He said in the
parables of the Sower (Matt. 13:1–23), Wheat and Tares (Matt. 13:
24–30, 36–43), and the Net (Matt. 13:47–50) that not all who appear
to belong to him actually do.

For these we must pray that somehow, by the hearing of the gospel,
they may be born again.

Chapter 3

WHAT IS
THE TASK OF
THE PASTOR?

God gives gifted men to his people to teach them and train them. In the Old Testament God said, "And I will give you pastors according to mine heart, which shall feed you with knowledge and understanding" (Jer. 3:15). In the New Testament, Paul wrote, "And (He) gave gifts unto men . . . some, apostles; and some prophets; and some, evangelists; and some, pastors and teachers (or pastor-teacher); for the perfecting (equipping) of the saints" (Ephesians 4:8,11,12).

Out of the shepherding life of the Hebrews God revealed the basic concepts of the task of the pastor. The word "pastor" means shepherd. Among the Hebrews, shepherding was a highly honorable occupation. The office of the chief shepherd was one of great trust and honor. Mesha, king of Moab, was a sheepmaster (2 Kings 3:4). David was a shepherd boy. Jesus is called "that great shepherd of the sheep" (Hebrews 13:20). He said, "I am the good shepherd: the good shepherd giveth his life for the sheep" (John 10:11).

A shepherd's chief responsibility is to feed and protect the sheep in order that the sheep may grow and reproduce other sheep. The flocks can multiply only as the shepherd properly functions. A shepherd leads the flock to pasture in the morning, tends them by day and folds (puts them in pens) and watches them at night. It was the shepherd's duty to count the sheep daily and he was held responsible for every lost one (Gen. 31:38,39; Exodus 22:12,13; Luke 2:8; John 10:1–16). This task was often arduous and dangerous. The shepherd had to contend with the heat of the day and the cold of the night.

(Gen. 31:40). Wild animals were a constant threat (1 Samuel 17:34). If the protection of the shepherd was taken away wolves came in and destroyed the sheep. If there was no guidance from the shepherd, the sheep lost their way and wondered out of the pasture to starve. In either case reproduction was made impossible because of the shepherd. *Sheep must have a shepherd; a church must have a pastor!* It is a noble call to be chosen of God to be a shepherd in His church.

A pastor's main task, by the very nature of his office and calling, is to shepherd the flock of God. Jesus commanded Peter to "feed my lambs . . . my sheep" (John 21:15,16,17). As Peter learned his responsibility, he shared the nature of the task:

"Tend, nurture, guard, guide and fold the flock of God that is (your responsibility), not by coercion or constraint, but willingly; not dishonorably motivated by the advantages and profits (belonging to the office) but eagerly and cheerfully. Not (as arrogant, dictatorial and overbearing persons) domineering over those in your charge, but being examples—patterns and models of Christian living—to the flock (the congregation)" (1 Peter 5:2,3). A pastor must feed, guide and guard the church. Failure to feed the church on the truth of God will cause it to starve. Failure to guide the church will cause it to lose it's direction.

It was because of the importance of the pastor having adequate time for prayer and Bible study that the office of the deacon was born. "Therefore select out from among yourselves, brethren, seven men of good and attested character and repute, full of the (Holy) Spirit and wisdom, whom we may assign to look after this business and duty but we will continue to devote ourselves steadfastly to prayer and the ministry of the word" (Acts 6:3,4).

It cannot be emphasized too strongly that the key to a church acquiring and maintaining a healthy spiritual climate lies in the leadership of the pastor. Through Bible-centered preaching and teaching he must feed the church. Through Spirit directed leadership he must guide the church. Through God given wisdom he must guard the church.

Basically his approach must be two-fold: to individuals, and to the group.

First, a pastor must discover the value of one. He must begin with individuals. Yet, at the same time, he must teach the multitude, the whole church family. Because it is impossible for a pastor to deal personally with every member of his congregation, he must have help from spiritually trained laymen. He could begin with his deacons and the Bible teachers of the church. Think what would happen in a church if every deacon and every Bible teacher worked closely with the pastor as assistant pastors: the pastor teaching and training the teachers and the teachers and deacons teaching and training the members.

Paul said to Timothy, "and the (instructions) which you heard from me, along with many witnesses, transmit and entrust (as a deposit) to reliable and faithful men who will be competent and qualified to teach others also" (2 Tim. 2:2). One multiplied into two; two multipled to four, and on and on until there was a multitude. It is important to notice that disciples are spoken of as having multiplied, while the Lord added *DAILY* to the church those who were being saved.

Luke tells us that the Christians in the first church in Jerusalem were soon scattered throughout the whole area of Judea and Samaria, EXCEPT THE APOSTLES (Acts 8:1). Why didn't the apostles go out? It seems evident that they remained behind to continue teaching and training those who were being saved and added to the church.

Jesus taught the multitude, but at the same time he gathered around him a small band of men. Into these men he poured his life and truth. He taught them how to live and work and witness. As a result they multiplied the Lord's work many times into the lives of others.

Luke tells us that Jesus called His twelve disciples together and gave them power and authority. Then He sent them to preach. They departed, and went through the towns, preaching the gospel. Sometime later the Lord appointed seventy others and sent them two by two into every city and place where He was going. (Luke 9:1–6; 10:1).

He began with one, Andrew. Soon, He added another, Peter, until the number was twelve. He sent out these twelve and they grew to seventy. Seventy were sent forth two by two and the church grew into a multitude.

Any pastor who will follow the basic principles of shepherding the flock of God will soon see the small band multiply into a multitude. One can become two; two can become four; four can become eight, until there is a multitude. Remember, it begins with one!

A pastor must set the example by his walk in Christ, his witness of Christ, and his work with others. *He will never lead* his people *to do that which he himself does not do.* Paul, writing to the church at Thessalonica, wrote, "For our (preaching of the) glad tidings (the Gospel) came to you not only in word, but also in (it's own inherent) power and in the Holy Spirit, and with great conviction and absolute certainty (on our part). *You know what kind of men we proved our- selves to be among you for your good.* And you (set yourselves to) become imitators of us and (through us) of the Lord Himself, for you welcomed our message in (spite of the) much persecution, with joy (inspired) of the Holy Spirit: So that you (thus) became a pattern to all the believers—those who adhere to, trust in and rely on Christ Jesus—in Macedonia and Achaia (most of Greece)" (1 Thess. 1:5–7).

In Ephesians 4:11–16, Paul reveals that all of the gifted men of the church, including the pastor-teacher, have as a basic objective the task of equipping the saints to do the work of ministering. It is not the pastor who is to do the ministering, it is the saints. The pastor is to shepherd, to equip the saints in order that they, the saints, might do the work of ministering in building up the body of Christ, the church.

Many pastors spend all their energies in doing the ministry of the church and the people are dying spiritually because they are not fed or guided. A pastor must not do the work which the believers are called to do. His task is to equip the believers through Bible centered preaching and teaching, to do the work of building up the church.

A pastor must understand that, although he is the pace-setter, he cannot do all the visiting, teaching, praying, he cannot do everything, and he must not feel guilty because he cannot. As pastor, he must fulfill his unique function to make it possible for believers to be able to produce other believers through the witness of their lives and lips. His task is to teach and train believers to become followers of the Lord Jesus in order that the Lord may make them into fishers of men (Matthew 4:19). This is total evangelism!

PART TWO

PROGRAM OF FOLLOW-UP
EVANGELISM

Chapter 4

NEW TESTAMENT
METHODS OF
FOLLOW-UP

There are four basic methods of follow-up evangelism in the New Testament: intercessory prayer, personal contact, sending a substitute, and the written letter.

One of the most essential methods of follow-up is *INTERCESSORY PRAYER*. Yet, it is perhaps the most neglected. It is absolutely necessary that we pray for babes in Christ to grow and develop in the Lord. Jesus prayed for His disciples. He said to Simon, "Satan has asked excessively that (all of) you be given up to him—out of the power and keeping of God—that he might sift (all of) you like grain, But I have prayed especially for you (Peter) that your (own) faith may not fail; and when you yourself have turned again, strengthen and establish your brethren" (Luke 22:31,32).

He not only prayed for the disciples then, He also prayed for all who would ever believe in Him. "I am praying for them. I am not praying (requesting) for the world; but for those You have given Me, for they belong to You. I do not ask that you will take them out of the world, but that You will keep and protect them from the evil (one). Sanctify them—purify, consecrete, separate them for Yourself, make them holy—by the Truth. Your Word is Truth. Neither for these alone do I pray—it is not for their sake only that I make this request—but also for all those who will ever come to believe in (trust, cling to, rely on) Me through their word and teaching" (John 17:9, 15,17,20).

For the church at Philippi, Paul prayed, "that your love may

43

abound yet more and more and extend to its fullest development in knowledge and all keen insight—that is, that your love may (display itself in) greater depth of acquaintance and more comprehensive discernment; so that you may surely learn to sense what is vital, and approve and prize what is excellent and of real value—recognizing the highest and the best, and distinguishing the moral differences; and that you may be untainted and pure and unerring and blameless, that—with hearts sincere and certain and unsullied—you may (approach) the day of Christ, not stumbling nor causing others to stumble" (Phil. 1:9,10).

For the Ephesian Christians, he prayed, "I bow my knees before the Father of our Lord Jesus Christ. May He grant you out of the rich treasury of His glory to be strengthened and reinforced with mighty power in the inner man by the (Holy) Spirit (Himself)—indwelling your innermost being and personality. May Christ through your faith (actually) dwell—settle down, abide, make His permanent home—in your hearts! May you be rooted deep in love and founded securely on love, that you may have the power and be strong to apprehend and grasp with all the saints (God's devoted people, the experience of that love) what is the breadth and length and height and depth (of it); (That you may really come) to know—practically, through experience for yourselves—the love of Christ, which far surpasses mere knowledge (without experience); that you may be filled (through all your being) unto all the fullness of God (that is) may have the richest measure of the divine Presence, and become a body wholly filled and flooded with God Himself!" (Eph. 3:14,16–19).

For the Roman Christians Paul was so concerned that he said: "I always mention you when at my prayers" (Rom. 1:9).

For the young Christians at Colossae, special prayer was made "that you may be filled with the full (deep and clear) knowledge of His will in all spiritual wisdom (that is, in comprehensive insight into the ways and purposes of God) and in understanding and discernment of spiritual things; that you may walk (live and conduct yourselves) in a manner worthy of the Lord, fully pleasing to Him and desiring to please Him in all things, bearing fruit in every good work and steadily growing and increasing in (and by) the knowledge of God—

with fuller, deeper and clearer insight, acquaintance and recognition" (Col. 1:9,10).

Notice how specifically Paul prayed for these Christians; that they would be strengthened inwardly by the indwelling Holy Spirit; that they would grow in their knowledge of Jesus Christ and understand the ways and purposes of God in order that they might walk in a manner fully pleasing to Him; that they would learn to approve that which is of real value in life; that their love would grow; that they would not stumble or cause another to stumble; and that they would be filled and flooded throughout all their being with the very Presence of God Himself.

A second basic New Testament method of follow-up is *person to person CONTACT.* Although the Apostles continuously prayed for their converts, they considered PERSONAL CONTACT and TIME WITH THEM the most essential key to effectively build up their lives in Christ. "(And we) continue to pray especially and with most intense earnestness night and day that we might see you *face to face* and mend and make good whatever may be imperfect and lacking in your faith" (1 Thess. 3:10).

"And after some time Paul said to Barnabas, come, let us go back and again visit and help and minister to the brethren in every town where we made known the message of the Lord, and see how they are getting along" (Acts 15:36).

(1) *By living example.* Those who are to do follow-up work are to be living examples before the young Christians committed to their care. They will find the success of their task depends largely upon doing and being what they are teaching others to do and be. The person who seeks to do follow-up work must be what he is trying to teach. Paul said, "Pattern after me, follow my example as I imitate and follow Christ" (1 Cor. 11:1).

Paul said to the Thessalonians, "You know what kind of men we proved (ourselves) to be among you for your good . . . And you (set yourselves to) become imitators of us and (through us) of the Lord Himself, for you welcomed our message" (1 Thess. 1:5,6).

To the Christians at Philippi, Paul said, "Practice what you have learned and received and heard and seen in me, and model your way of living on it" (Phil. 4:9).

(2) By *individual instruction*. Paul and Barnabas ". . . made disciples of many of the people . . . establishing and strengthening the souls and the hearts of the disciples, urging and warning and encouraging them to stand firm in the faith" (Acts 14:21,22).

Paul told the Thessalonians, "You learned from us about how you ought to walk so as to please and gratify God, as indeed you are doing; that you do so ever more and more abundantly—attaining yet greater perfection in liveing this life" (1 Thess. 4:1).

"And the (instructions) which you have heard from me, along with many witnesses, transmit and entrust (as a deposit) to reliable and faithful men who will be competent and qualified to teach others also" (2 Tim. 2:2).

"Him we preach and proclaim, warning and admonishing every one and instructing every one in all wisdom, (in comprehensive insight into the ways and purposes of God) that we may present every person mature—full-grown, fully initiated, complete and perfect—in Christ, the anointed one" (Col. 1:28).

(3) By *group fellowship*. Individuals must become a part of the group fellowship of the church if they are to maintain their Christian growth. Fellowship describes the New Testament church more than any other characteristic. In fact, it was often called "the fellowship." "Therefore, those who accepted and welcomed his message were baptized and there were added that day about three thousand souls. And they steadfastly persevered, devoting themselves constantly to the instruction and fellowship of the apostles, to the breaking of bread (including the Lord's Supper) and prayers" (Acts 2:41,42).

SENDING A SUBSTITUTE

When the disciples were unable to go personally, they would send another to take their place. A pastor cannot deal with everyone. But he can send another. Send them! Don't expect them to go on their own. If they don't know to go they won't.

"But since we were bereft of you, brethren, for a little while in person, (of course) not in heart, we endeavored the more eagerly and with great longing to see you face to face . . . Therefore, when (the suspense of separation and our yearning for some personal communication from you) became intolerable . . . we sent Timothy, our brother and God's servant in (spreading) the good news (the Gospel) of Christ, to strengthen and establish, exhort and comfort and encourage you in your faith" (1 Thess. 2:17, 3:1,2).

"But I hope and trust in the Lord Jesus soon to send Timothy to you, so that I may also be encouraged and cheered by learning news of you. For I have no one like him—no one of so kindred a spirit—who will be so genuinely interested in your welfare and devoted to your interests. For the others all seek (to advance) their own interests, not those of Jesus Christ, the Messiah. But Timothy's tested worth you know, how as a son with his father he has toiled with me zealously (serving and helping to advance) the good news (the Gospel). I hope therefore to send him promptly just as soon as I know how my case is going to turn out. But (really) I am confident and fully trusting in the Lord that shortly I myself shall come to you also" (Phil. 2:19–24).

CONTACT BY OTHER MEANS OF COMMUNICATION

If it were impossible for the disciples to go personally to care for the converts, or to send another, they contacted them by other means. A written letter was one of the chief methods in the New Testament times.

Today, we too can utilize many means of communication to keep in contact with young believers. A written letter, telephone call, tapes of sermons, films or filmstrips, slides, or some other media may be used to instruct and strengthen the new Christian. Much of the New Testament, especially Paul's writings, was written as follow-up instructions to young converts.

"(Mark carefully these closing words of mine) See with what large letters I am writing them with my own hand" (Gal. 6:11).

"I do not write this to shame you, but to warn and counsel you as my beloved children" (1 Cor. 4:14).

"My little children, I write you these things so that you may not violate God's law and sin–. . ." (1 John 2:1).

In summary: Paul said, "I have become all things to all men, that I might by all means . . . . save some . . . . and this I do for the Gospel's sake . . . that I might become a participator in it and share in its (blessings along with you") (1 Cor. 9:22,23).

Chapter 5

DECISION
COUNSELING
PROGRAM

In any person's life the most crucial moment is the time of his decision to accept Jesus Christ as Savior. Heaven and Hell, life and death are involved.

Realizing it is impossible for the pastor to adequately deal with those coming forward during an invitation because of the brief time and the pressure of the onlooking congregation, the need has been felt to use trained workers to assist the pastor in a personal and private way.

"Decision Counseling" is a specialized program using a few trained workers to help the pastor in counseling and guiding those making decisions during the services of the church. In most churches this group could come from the deacons and their wives, or from the Sunday School workers. They must be especially trained for this important task.

Billy Graham has said that one of the great weaknesses of evangelism lies at this point. The question he faced was, how could persons be persuaded to make a profession of faith, or indicate their spiritual need, and to do it properly so that each one would be dealt with personally and adequately? The Graham team considers that mass evangelism merely sets the stage for personal evangelism and that it must become personal, if it is to be effective. They have discovered that the many people who come forward are not all finders. Many of them are still seekers. They are inquiring; they are seeking help; they need someone to guide them and lead them and direct them.

Some feel that only a minister can do that. However, the early church was made up of laymen who ministered to the needs of the members. In fact, Paul said that the pastor of the church is to equip the laymen to do the work of ministering to the church, so that all are built up in Christ (Eph. 4:11–16). THE LAYMEN SHOULD BE IN THE WORK OF EVANGELISM GIVING MEANING TO THE PASTOR'S INVITATION by following up inquirers with personal guidance.

A COUNSELING ROOM: MATERIALS AND ARRANGEMENTS

1. A Counseling Room near the auditorium should be prepared. Chairs should be arranged in pairs—one counselor to one inquirer. A layman should be in charge of the Counseling Room and should see that it is prepared before each service. He should be elected by the church and could be called the "Director of Follow-Up."

2. A Decision Card, selected Bible study guides, and counseling helps selected by the church should be placed on each pair of seats. The Bible study booklet, *Your Life In Christ,* published by Broadman Press, has been especially prepared to be used with those making decisions.

3. A quiet atmosphere is to be maintained in the Counseling Room at all times.

THREE BASIC THINGS A DECISION COUNSELOR MUST DO AT THE TIME OF DECISION

1. Help make certain the inquirer is clear as to his decision.
   (1) The individual cannot properly build an abundant life on a shaky foundation of understanding.
   (2) Some will have made their decision during the service.
   (3) Some will confess they do not remember much of the sermon, but felt drawn of the Lord to move forward.
   (4) Each is an individual with individual problems and must be dealt with accordingly. ·
2. Begin follow-up immediately.
   (1) Satan will attack immediately with doubt, temptations and discouragement

(2) These spiritual infants need IMMEDIATE CARE.
   a. They have been born into God's family as babes in Christ (1 Peter 2:2)
   b. These spiritual infants need to be FED, PROTECTED and TRAINED (1 Cor. 4:15).
   c. The counselor gives the "first bottle of spiritual milk" (John 21:15).
3. Secure accurate information on the Decision Card.

PROCEDURES IN DECISION COUNSELING

DURING THE INVITATION

1. The counselor may sit anywhere but preferably on an aisle and near the front of the auditorium.

2. As the invitation begins, a few Decision Counselors, both men and women, should come quickly to the front of the auditorium and be seated. This will make them available as decisions are made. Until decisions are made they should spend these moments in a prayerful attitude.

3. The counselor must watch the pastor as unobtrusively as possible. If someone comes forward, a counselor is to rise and stand quietly beside the pastor as he talks to the inquirer. The counselor must not speak until the pastor introduces him to the inquirer.

4. After the pastor introduces the counselor to the inquirer, the counselor will take him immediately to the counseling room and seek to meet his need.

HOW TO HELP THE INQUIRER IN THE COUNSELING ROOM

I. Get Acquainted

1. Be seated quickly and get acquainted.

2. Write his name on the Decision Card so it can be used in conversation. Do not complete the card until after the interview.

3. Seek to put him at ease immediately. Assure him that his friends or parents are waiting for him.

4. If the inquirer is in a hurry, take that into consideration. Do not detain him unnecessarily. Courtesy and thoughtfulness always!

II. Determine the Need of the Inquirer

Remember to rely on the Holy Spirit; to pray quietly for guidance; to look for the basic need. (The inquirer may think his need is to get over some habit, but the real need may be salvation.) Remember to listen carefully. A good counselor is a good listener.

1. Begin by encouraging the inquirer to express himself by asking questions. Do not do all the talking! Following are a few suggestions:

    (1) "Why have you come forward?"

    (2) "What did you have in mind as you came forward?"

    (3) "What decision are you making?"

2. Avoid any arguments (2 Tim. 2:24). Never directly contradict any statement he may give—or tell him, "You're wrong!" Maintain a positive attitude. Seek to be understanding. Point him to Jesus through the Scripture.

3. Some will have made their decisions during the message. If so, make certain the decision is clear and lead him to have assurance.

III. Meet the Need

Remember to rely on the Holy Spirit; to avoid arguments; to refuse prying (Proverbs 11:13).

1. Use the open Bible. God has promised to honor His Word, not our arguments. It is preferable to let the inquirer look on as verses are read to him. Don't use too many verses as this can confuse.

2. Introduce the inquirer to Christ. Do not try to bring him to some emotional or mystical experience. Feelings and emotions are a vital part of the Christian life, but they do not bring salvation. Salvation is by grace through faith in Christ. Help him come to Christ, Who alone saves, lifts burdens, strengthens the life, etc. Magnify Jesus Christ.

3. Do not overly persuade him to make a decision. Let him wait if he is not ready now. If he doesn't make a decision now, leave the door open for further counsel by courtesy and thoughtfulness.

IV. Lead the Inquirer to Pray

1. Once a decision is ready to be made, the counselor should lead in a prayer. He should ask God to guide the inquirer in his decision.

2. Then lead him to pray

    (1) Kneel if he so desires.

    (2) It is good if he will pray aloud, but don't unduly force.

    (3) If he doesn't know what to pray, suggest a simple prayer for him to follow, but be careful that he doesn't simply repeat words.

    (4) If he is trusting Christ as Saviour, instruct him to pray and ask

Christ to come into his life.

(5) If he is a Christian seeking to yield his life anew to Christ, or seeking strength and guidance, etc., instruct him to confess his sins to God and claim God's promise that He will forgive my sins" (1 John 1:9).

3. After the inquirer has prayed, the counselor should lead in a prayer of thanksgiving.

V. Then, Establish Assurance

1. Talk with him briefly about his decision.
   (1) Ask how he knows he is saved. See that he stands on the Word of God for assurance. The great temptation is to put one's faith in his feeling, which is not the proper foundation of assurance. Use 1 John 5:11,12. God promised to save us if we come to Him in faith. We must stand by faith and trust upon what God said He would do.
   (2) Ask if everything is settled now.
   (3) If the counselor is unable to meet his need, consult the Director of Follow-up, or the pastor. Recognize that there are limitations of a decision counselor. Do not hesitate to seek help.

2. After this, FILL IN A DECISION CARD completely and legibly. This is extremely important.
   (1) Fill in the card normally. If the individual is emotionally upset, handle the situation as personably and understandingly as possible. (Each counselor should fill in a decision card for practice.)
   (2) The counselor will double-check the information on the card and give it to the Director of Follow-up before leaving.

VI. Explain and Emphasize the Follow-Up Lessons

1. Give the individual the Bible study booklet, "Your Life In Christ," provided by the church and *EXPLAIN* the method of study used in these follow-up lessons. If "Your Life In Christ" is used, explain that he is simply to look up the scripture reference and then, as nearly as possible, answer the question in his own words. It would be good to have him answer the first question in Chapter 1 to make sure he understands.

2. *EMPHASIZE* the tremendous importance of hiding God's Word in the heart for strength in meeting the doubts and discouragements the individual will immediately face.

3. *GIVE* him a church brochure, if available, to acquaint him with the activities and ministries of the church.

VII. HE WILL BE PRESENTED TO THE CHURCH

1. Inform him that the pastor will present him to the church to be approved for baptism and/or church membership. WHEN this is to be done is optional. It must be determined by the local church.

2. Some have their order of service arranged so that the announcements, and offering come AFTER the invitation, thus allowing the counselors time to deal with each decision. The individual is brought back into the service and presented to the church at the conclusion. If the counselor does not complete his work, the individual is presented at the very next service he attends.

3. *Others,* with a regular order of service, simply present the individual at the very next service he attends. A special card, such as a duplicate Decision Card, or a simple white card, could be filled out and given to the individual to bring back and give to the pastor at the time he comes before the church explaining his decision. This would enable the pastor to realize that he has already come forward for counseling and now needs to be presented to the church.

If he is not presented at the time of his decision, seek to get a definite commitment about the next service which he will attend (Acts 2:41). It is basic that he be lead to confess with his mouth that Jesus is now his Saviour and Lord.

DECISION COUNSELOR'S HOME VISIT WITH SUNDAY SCHOOL WORKER

After we have done all that we have discussed, our responsibility to the one who made a decision has only begun.

Our objective is to see not only that the lost are converted; the doubtful strengthened, etc., but also that they are going on with Christ in the life of the church and community.

If these new Christians and church members are to go on to become mature, useful, fruitful Christians, then they must be spiritually fed, protected, and trained. This is our Lord's Great Commission to the Church (Matt. 28:18–20). Paul spoke of this in Ephesians 4:11–16 as the major responsibility of every Christian in the church.

We already have an excellent organization to accomplish this task in the Sunday School Bible study program. We do not need additional organization, but only to more effectively use what we have.

A Sunday School class is designed to involve the individual. The teacher can deal individually with each person in the class and involve the individual in the group.

A Sunday School worker will usually have the person from six months to a full year. What he does in teaching and training this individual about the Christian Life may mean the difference in years of delightful victory or frustrating defeat. *However, before this program can achieve the objectives of teaching and training new believers, EVERY teacher must himself be trained in the ministry of follow-up work.* Businesses spend millions of dollars yearly to train their workers. Surely a church can do no less to equip its workers to do the most important work on the earth.

1. Follow-up begins with effective *DECISION COUNSELING* by the one leading the individual to Christ. It may be the pastor, a counselor, or friend. It may be at the conclusion of a worship service, in a home, or even at work.

2. Follow-up must continue with a Sunday School worker making an *Initial 48 Hour Visit* after the decision. It is suggested that the Decision Counselor accompany the Sunday School worker on this visit. A card could be given or mailed to the Sunday School worker assigning him this responsibility.

A Sample *INITIAL VISIT CARD*

(1) The *first* purpose of this visit will be to become personally acquainted.

Even though the teacher may already know the new member, and even if the new member has belonged to and attended the Sunday School it is still important that this INITIAL VISIT be made. The Sunday School teacher must show a genuine interest. He must personally get to know and love the person. He should pray daily that, as a teacher, there will be a growing love and understanding. He must never, never let this simply become a duty. The teacher must be a good listener. An excellent way of showing sincere interest in another person is to ask questions which will draw him out and get him to share. Arguments should be avoided. Arguments only build walls of misunderstanding.

When working with children, the teacher must cultivate a proper relationship with the parents, especially those who are not Christians or members of the church. He will want to help them understand that he is not taking over their responsibility of spiritual guidance in the home.

(2) A *second* purpose will be to give further assurance and instruction to the new Christian concerning his decision. The Bible study booklet, *Your Life in Christ,* has been prepared to be used as a study guide with the new member.

(3) A *third* purpose is to encourage the new member to be faithful in attending Sunday School and the worship services of the church.

3. A counselor's continuing responsibility will be to check on the progress of the individual.

(1) A check can be made by looking at the Individual Sunday School Record Card kept in the church office.

(2) Additional visits (at least twice)'should be made with the Sunday School worker during an extensive follow-up period of 10–12 weeks.

(3) If difficulties arise and the individual needs help which neither the counselor nor the Sunday School worker is able to give, IMMEDIATE HELP should be sought from the director of follow-up, pastor, or a deacon.

(4) Follow-up will continue for a lifetime through all the ministries of the church.

PRACTICAL HELPS IN DEALING WITH DIFFERENT DECISIONS

Basic Decisions

* Acceptance of Christ as Saviour—a first-time commitment to Christ.

* Assurance of Salvation—a problem of doubt has arisen regarding a previous experience.

* Restoration of Fellowship—A Christian who comes forward because of

carelessness, indifference, specific sins, etc.

* Transfer of Membership—a Baptist moving his membership into this church by letter or statement.

* Special Service or Seeking God's will—a person living his life into a full-time Christian vocation or one coming, seeking to find the will of God for his life.

DETAILED TREATMENT

Acceptance of Christ as Saviour

1. Begin by saying, "Let's see what God's word has to say about how you can invite Jesus into your life."

2. Present the gospel—There are many excellent tools available. Every Decision Counselor should use the method which is natural for him. Ask the pastor for suggested helps.

Assurance of Salvation

1. Make certain the inquirer understands the fundamentals of the gospel. Go over a brief presentation with him.

2. Show what God's Word says about assurance of salvation.
   (1) We must not trust in feelings (2 Cor. 5:7).
   (2) We can know and be certain (1 John 5:13, 2:3–5; 3:14; 4:13; John 3:36).
   (3) We must stand upon the promise, integrity and ability of God (John 10:27–29; Rom. 8:35–39).

3. When the way of salvation seems to be clear, then ask him to tell how he knows he is a Christian.

Restoration of Fellowship

1. Point to the cause of broken fellowship (Isaiah 59:1,2; 1 Peter 3:12).

2. Show that God is ready to forgive and on what basis (1 John 1:9; Proverbs 28:13).

3. Instruct him in the way of a victorious walk (1 Cor. 10:13; 1 John 4:4).
   (1) Urge the importance of a daily prayer time (Matt. 26:41).
   (2) Show the necessity of a daily Bible study (Acts 17:11; Matt. 4:4; Psalm 119:11).
   (3) Stress the importance of fellowship with other believers in the church by regular, faithful church attendance (Heb. 10:25).

Special Service or Seeking God's Will

1. Stress the major will of God for everyone. We begin to do God's will by doing the things we know to do. God's major will is that we walk in Him and witness of Him. We are to know Him and make Him known. God wills that every Christian be surrendered and separated (1 Thess. 4:3–7). This we know God wants us to do. God wills that every Christian be His witness to the world. Whether businessman, student, etc., we are to be His witnesses (Acts 1:8). This we know God wants us to do.

2. Now point out that God has a specific area of life in which we are to do this major task. There isn't any satisfaction outside His will. God's will can be defeated by our own decision to refuse to be completely SURRENDERED and SEPARATED. But we can find God's will and act upon it. His will is always best for us.

3. Point out that God's specific will is often revealed to us in steps. Until we have taken one step, God will not reveal the next. In seeking God's will, we may find the following steps of guidance helpful.

   (1) Desire—Point out that this must come after surrender and separation or it will be a selfish desire.

   (2) Ability—God will give us the ability to do what He demands.

   (3) Opportunity—God will always open doors of opportunity to do His will.

4. Help him to seek the attitude of Jesus, "Not my will, but (always) Yours, be done" (Luke 22:42). (See also Phil. 2:5–13.)

Transfer of Membership

The person transferring his membership can be counseled at the front of the auditorium or in the counseling room. This should be one of the finest moments in the life of a person finding a new church home. The local church must decide which procedure it will follow.

1. The counselor should begin by briefly giving a testimony about what the church means to him. Help the new member (or family) feel warmly welcomed and wanted.

2. Challenge him (or the family) concerning the importance of his new church membership. The counselor should let him know that he wants to be of any help and assistance he can.

3. Stress, briefly, the importance of daily Bible study, prayer, and faithfulness in church attendance. This can best be done through the personal testimony about what these mean in the life of the counselor.

Dealing with Inactive Members

One of the greatest problems facing the average church is the number of inactive members among the membership. The basic principles of Follow-up can be used to reclaim some of these for the Lord. As a teacher discovers someone in his class who is habitually absent, he may approach him in the following way and seek to meet his needs.

A Simple Approach

TEACHER: "Tell me, when did you come to know Christ as your Saviour? Was it in a revival, regular service, or in your home? Did someone personally deal with you? Do you remember how you felt before? After?" (You are striving to get the individual to think back about his conversion experience. If he reveals that he has never been converted, give your testimony and invite him to receive Christ.)

TEACHER: "In your mind, what do you think a person has to do to be a happy Christian?" (Most will give the correct answers.)

TEACHER: Are you as happy now as when you first received Christ into your heart? or "Has being a Christian meant as much to you as you thought it would?" (You are endeavoring to get the individual to see his spiritual condition and desire help.)

TEACHER: "Would you mind if I shared with you how I found happiness in my Christian life." (One of the best methods of giving an individual guidance is by sharing your experience with him.)

"I've discovered that one of the most basic things we need to do is study the Bible. It is the spiritual food we need by which to grow. You see, just as we need physical food to grow, we also need spiritual food to grow."

"Most of us know this, but we may not know HOW to study the Bible so that it makes sense and helps us. For a long time I didn't know how to read or study the Bible. Maybe you have felt the same way."

"Well our church has some Bible studies which help a person to know how to study the Bible in an interesting way so that it makes sense and means something. I'd like to leave one with you. Look through it. I think you'll find it as helpful and interesting as I have. (Leave the booklet, *Your Life inn Christ.*) I hope you'll be back with us soon and share with us in Bible study."

A Practical Suggestion

Perhaps a growing, mature class member could be assigned to look after this "inactive member" for several weeks.

General Helps on Follow-Up Instruction

* TELL HIM WHY!
—Needs to attend church
—Needs to study the Bible
—Needs to pray
—Needs to witness
* SHOW HIM HOW!
—To worship in the church
—To study the Bible
—To pray
—To witness
* GET HIM STARTED!
—Attending church regularly
—Studying the Bible daily
—Spending time in prayer daily
—Witnessing as he has opportunity
* KEEP HIM GOING—CHECK HIS PROGRESS
—In church attendance
—In daily Bible study
—In daily prayer
—In personal witnessing, helping him to lead another to Christ
* HELP HIM HELP ANOTHER
—To get started attending church
—To begin personal Bible study
—To establish a prayer life
—To witness to a lost friend

BY WAY OF REVIEW

WHAT IS DONE IN THE COUNSELING ROOM?

1. Decision Counselor is to be seated quickly and get acquainted.
2. Determine the NEED of the inquirer.
   (1) Encourage him to express himself by asking questions. Do not do all the talking.
   (2) Look for the basic need.
   (3) Quietly pray for wisdom and guidance.
3. Meet the need with the OPEN BIBLE. Point the inquirer to Christ.

4. Lead the inquirer to pray.
5. Establish assurance. Fill in the Decision Card.
6. Explain and emphasize the follow-up lesson booklet.
7. Turn in the Decision Card before leaving.

WHAT IS THE CONTINUING RESPONSIBILITY?

1. Make the initial 48 hour visit to the home (Sunday School Bible teacher and Decision Counselor).
2. Continue to pray and be concerned for the individual.
3. Involve the new member into the fellowship of the church.

Chapter 6

STEPS
TOWARD
INVOLVEMENT

Involvement! This is the key. A new Christian, or new member, who is not involved will soon be lost for the cause of Christ, and the most crucial time in the new Christian's life is the first few days and weeks following his conversion. He is like a new born babe that doesn't know how to walk, talk, or feed himself. Therefore, he doesn't know what to do, say, or what he needs to live.

It is absolutely essential that he receives individual counsel and instruction during this time.

There are at least five basic, immediate needs for the new Christian.

(1) New Christians must be helped to have a definite assurance of salvation to combat doubt and discouragement caused by Satan.

(2) They must be shown how to study the Bible and taught to be obedient to God's word. Merely giving them Bible study materials and telling them it is important will not do. They must be shown how and then challenged to start. Follow-up work is done by SOMEONE, not by something.

(3) New Christians must be led to develop habits of daily prayer by personally praying with them and giving them suggestions about how to pray. Even the early disciples had to ask Jesus to teach them how to pray (Luke 11:1).

(4) They must be guided to attend church faithfully, and taught to worship God properly and intelligently.

(5) New Christians, and most new members, must be trained to witness by life and word as they are helped to formulate their personal testimony to share with others. They need to be given "on-the-job" training by being taken on witnessing visits by Sunday School teacher, pastor, or deacon.

Any church that is to be successful in follow-up work must be thoroughly convinced of these needs and determined to meet them at all cost.

Basically, the follow-up ministry in a church is a two-fold approach: the individual and group. Both of these approaches are essential, and each is dependent upon the other.

The *Individual Approach* will primarily involve the Sunday School Bible teacher, and include the pastor and staff, deacons, training leaders, and other individuals who are in a position to give personal guidance. But the Bible teacher is the *KEY PERSON*.

We do not need additional organization to minister to the new member but rather to utilize the present organizations of the church. And it is the Sunday School Bible study program which is the *FOUNDATIONAL ORGANIZATION* for follow-up. But the workers must be given *DIRECTION* and *MOTIVATION* if the work is to be done.

A Sunday School Bible teacher will normally have the members of his class for approximately one year. In some cases he will have them longer. In most instances he will have them even less. What the Bible teacher does in teaching and training the new Christian during this time may mean the difference in a life of victory or defeat.

The *GROUP APPROACH* will involve the new member classes, Sunday School Bible study classes, Christian Life and Service Training groups, the worship services, and other groups within the fellowship of the church.

STEPS TOWARD PERSONAL INVOLVEMENT

After twenty years of pastoring, thirteen in his present church, this author has found the following steps to be the most helpful in involving new Christians and new members into the fellowship of the church. Some of these steps occur simultaneously.

A survey was made of several Christian leaders (pastors, ministers of education, professors of religious education, pastoral counseling, and theology) about these basic steps and it was concluded that these areas are of utmost priority in ministering to the needs of new Christians. It is hoped that they will be of practical value to every church seeking to minister to new Christians and new members.

Step Number One: EFFECTIVE DECISION COUNSELING

Begin with effective DECISION COUNSELING, and effective decision counseling is done by trained workers. Only eternity will reveal how many lives have been lost to the cause of Christ because the claims of Christ were so carelessly presented at the time of decision. When Jesus calls a man to follow Him he asks him to count the cost. He challenges a person to *deny* himself and *depend* fully upon Him. For us to be unclear in presenting Christ's claims is to plant seeds for future confusion and frustration.

A new Christian cannot properly build a successful life upon a shaky foundation. He must understand clearly how to accept Christ and what the Lord expects of him from that moment forward. This subject is dealt with in detail in Chapter 5, "Decision Counseling Program".

STEP NUMBER TWO: AN INITIAL 48 HOUR VISIT

Within 48 hours following the time of decision a counselor and Sunday School teacher should visit the new Christian or member in his home. The purpose of this visit is for fellowship and further spiritual instruction. A more detailed study of the purposes of this visit are outlined in Chapter 5, "Decision Counseling Program."

STEP NUMBER THREE: Pastor's Welcome Hour

This is a time when the pastor meets with those who have joined the church to share with them about the church and its ministry. It may involve an individual, family, or group. It is a one hour, one time, session. It may be done weekly, bi-weekly, or even monthly. It could be done during the Sunday School hour or during the week. As a pastor, this author has found Sunday morning during the Sunday School hour to be the best time. An intensive effort is made to get the new member to come to this class the very next Sunday after he has joined. If a family has joined the whole family, members or not, is encouraged to attend. It could be held in the pastor's study or an available classroom or even in a member's home.

This time has proven to be one of the most beneficial functions for welcoming the new member and getting him involved of all the programs suggested.

The primary purpose of this hour is two-fold:

(1) First purpose is to draw out of the new Christian, or member, a testimony about his life. This will enable the pastor to become more personally acquainted with each new member. This may be done with a few simple questions. It has been found helpful for everyone in the group to be allowed

to answer each question before moving to the next.

    (a) "Tell me about your life before you were saved; where you were born
       .. . grew up . . . went to school . . ."
    (b) "Tell me about when you first began thinking about your need for
       Christ . . . when you received Christ. Where were you? How did
       you feel? What did you think? What did you ask Christ to do?"
    (c) "How has Christ changed your life since you received Him . . . at
       home, school, or work . . . in the problems you face, in your plans,
       in your feelings toward yourself and others?"

(2) A second purpose of this hour is for the pastor to close with a clear
statement as to the objectives and ministries of the church. He must reserve
enough time to do this at the close.

Every effort should be made to get 100% attendance. A letter from the
pastor on Monday, after someone has joined, inviting them to be present the
very next Sunday is extremely helpful. A personal telephone call from the
pastor a day or so before Sunday is also encouraging. The Decision Counselor
and the Sunday School teacher should encourage the new member to attend
this welcome class when they make the Initial Visit in the home earlier in
the week.

STEP NUMBER FOUR: Bible Survey Class

Often one of the most frustrating experiences of the new Christian is to
be put into a Bible study group to start studying the Bible which he knows
nothing about.

It has been felt for years that one of the most essential needs of the new
Christian is to have a brief Bible survey course to acquaint him with the Bible
which he is to spend a lifetime studying. Our Christian universities and
seminaries have this as a basic requirement. Why can't the church at least
teach a general overview of the Bible to it's members? This author has
developed a graded (children, youth, and adult) pictorial overview of the
Bible to be taught over a 6 to 8 week period. It is taught on Sunday morning
during the Sunday School hour. Then, the new member is transfered into his
regular Bible study class. It has had remarkable success. Materials for this
class may be obtained from several sources. *The Bible Survey Series,* Convention Press, is excellent resource material. There are also pictorial Bible
surveys available. A pictorial overview has been found to be of great value
in introducing the unfolding message of the Bible.

STEP NUMBER FIVE: Christian Life Class

The purpose of this class is to acquaint the new Christian with the basics of the Christian life. This class could be offered on Sunday evenings during the training time at the same time the Bible survey class is being taught to new members on Sunday mornings. Thus every Sunday for 6 to 8 weeks he will be studying a survey of the Bible in the morning and how to live a Christian life in the evenings. The Bible study booklet, *Your Life in Christ,* Broadman Press, could be used as a study guide for this class. It deals with the six foundational issues of the Christian life: Christ Living in You; A Life of Victory, Christian Fellowship for Your Life, The Prayer Filled Life, God's Word in Your Life, and Witnessing—Sharing Your Life.

This class may be graded into children youth, and adult groups or any practical combination. Adequate trained leaders will need to be enlisted.

STEP NUMBER SIX: Sunday School Bible Study Class

This is the *heart* of the follow-up program of a church. God's truth is the spiritual food which is absolutely necessary for spiritual growth, and it is the Sunday School program in a church which is given the responsibility of teaching the Bible. Therefore The *KEY ORGANIZATION* is the Sunday School. The *KEY MAN* in the follow-up program is the Sunday School Bible teacher. Therefore, he must have a clean vision of this work. Where there is no vision a people will perish (Prov. 29:18). This principle also applies to a Bible study class. If a teacher does not have a clear vision of his purpose and responsibility, a class will perish. It is so important that the principles of this person-to-person ministry be constantly kept before the Bible teacher.

A Bible teacher's objective is two-fold;

(1) To *Teach* men the *will* of God.

(2) To *Train* men to *witness* of the Lord.

When Ananias dealt with Paul these two objectives were clearly revealed: "The God of our forefathers has destined and appointed you to come progressively to *know His will* . . . For you will *be His witness* unto all men of everything that you have seen and heard" (Acts 22:14,15).

A Bible study class must grow in its knowledge of God's will. But it also needs to reach out with its witness to others, win them to Christ, and bring them together for teaching and training. A class that will discover God's will, will go out witnessing to God's world.

THIS IS FOLLOW-UP EVANGELISM.

STEP NUMBER SEVEN: Christian Service Training

After the new member completes the Christian Life Class offered on Sunday evenings, he should be enrolled in the church training program. Through this program he is trained for Christian service and ministry for his entire lifetime. His training has helped him discover: How to walk in Christ; How to witness of Christ; and How to work with others in Christ. Every Christian is to be a missionary and his mission field is wherever he is. So, involve every believer in walking in Christ, in witnessing of Christ, and working with those who trust Christ as Saviour, so that they may learn to walk in Christ, witness of Christ, and work with others. THIS IS FOLLOW-UP EVANGELISM.

BY WAY OF REVIEW

1st Step—Effective Decision Counseling
2nd Step—Initial 48 Hour Home Visit
3rd Step—Pastor's Fellowship Hour
4th Step—Bible Survey Class
5th Step—Christian Life Class
6th Step—Sunday School Bible Study Class
7th Step—Christian Service Training Groups

PART THREE

PERSONAL PREPARATION
FOR FOLLOW-UP EVANGELISM

A person who seeks to do follow-up work must be and do what he teaches another to be and do. He must walk in Christ himself, if he is to show another how to walk in Christ (Phil. 4:9).

Chapter 7

HOW TO START
A PERSONAL
BIBLE STUDY

God's word teaches us to search for the wisdom of God as we would for HIDDEN TREASURE (Prov. 2:4). David said, "I love thy commandments above gold, yea above fine gold" (Psalm 119:127). We are to "receive the word with readiness of mind, and SEARCH THE SCRIPTURES, daily" (Acts 17:11).

This precious treasure is our spiritual food so necessary if we are to grow and develop as Christians. Peter said, "Like newborn babies you should crave—thirst for, earnestly desire—the pure (unadulterated) spiritual milk, that by it you may be nurtured and grow unto (completed) salvation" (I Peter 2:2). We take time to feed ourselves physically; we must also take time to feed ourselves spiritually (Job 23:12).

The word of God is also a light that guides our daily walk with Christ. The Psalmist said, "Thy word is a lamp unto my feet, and a light unto my path" (Psalm 119:105). Set aside a regular time each day to study God's Word.

I. WHY STUDY THE BIBLE?

1. *Helps us to discover Christ personally as we walk in Him each day.*

"You search and investigate and pore over the Scriptures diligently . . . And these (very Scriptures) testify about Me!" (John 5:39).

"The person who has My commands and keeps them is the one who (really) loves Me, and whoever (really) loves Me will be loved

73

by My Father. And I (too) will love him and will show (reveal, manifest) Myself to him—I will let Myself be clearly seen by him and make Myself real to him" (John 14:21).

2. *Nourishes us with spiritual food for growing.*

"Like newborn babies you should crave—thirst for, earnestly desire—the pure (unadulterated) spiritual milk, that by it you may be nurtured and grow unto (completed) salvation" (1 Peter 2:2).

"But He replied, It has been written, Man shall not live and be upheld and sustained by bread alone, but by every word that comes forth from the mouth of God (Deut. 8:3)" (Matt. 4:4).

"How sweet are thy words unto my taste! yea, sweeter than honey to my mouth" (Psalm 119:103).

"Neither have I gone back from the commandment of his lips; I have esteemed the words of his mouth more than my necessary food" (Job 23:12).

3. *Gives us spiritual power against yielding to temptation.*

"Wherewithal shall a young man cleanse his way? by taking heed thereto according to thy word. Thy word have I hid in mine heart, that I might not sin against thee" (Psalm 119:9,11) (KJV).

4. *Gives us spiritual light for walking the proper path of life.*

"Thy word is a lamp unto my feet, and a light unto my path" (Ps. 119:105) (KJV).

5. *Give us spiritual armor for victory in the battle against sin and Satan.*

"Put on God's whole armor—the armor of a heavy-armed soldier, which God supplies—that you may be able successfully to stand up against all the strategies and the deceits of the devil" (Eph. 6:11). (See also Eph. 6:12–17.)

6. *Instructs us in the truth of God.*

"Every Scripture is God-breathed—given by His inspiration—and profitable for instruction, for reproof and conviction of sin, for correction of error and discipline in obedience, and for training in righteousness that is, in holy living, in conformity to God's will in thought, purpose and action. So that the man of God may be complete and proficient, well-fitted and thoroughly equipped for every good work" (2 Tim. 3:16,17).

7. *Fills our heart with something to witness to others.*

"Then I said, I will not make mention of him, nor speak any more in his name. But his word was in mine heart as a burning fire shut up in my bones, and I was weary with forbearing, and I could not stay (remain silent)" (Jer. 20:9) (KJV).

"But in your hearts set Christ apart as holy (and acknowledge Him) as Lord. Always be ready to give a logical defense to any one who asks you to account for the hope that is in you, but do it courteously and respectfully (Isa. 8:12,13)" (1 Peter 3:15).

"I will speak of thy testimonies also before kings, and will not be ashamed" (Psalm 119:46) (KJV).

II. HOW TO STUDY THE BIBLE?

PRINCIPLES OF BIBLE STUDY

1. *Begin with prayer.*

"Give me understanding, that I may learn thy commandments" (Psalm 119:73) (KJV).

2. *Study from the Bible itself.*

First we need to do some personal, original investigation into the passage. We need to allow the Holy Spirit to instruct us in the truth of God's Word. The Bible best explains itself, if the Spirit is guiding. Other aids may be used—but it is important that we study the inspired Word itself.

3. *Use helpful Bible study tools.*

What Bible study tools are needed? The basics are: Two or more good translations, a Bible dictionary, and a good Concordance.

4. *Study systematically.*

Begin with the *Your Life in Christ* Bible study booklet. The Sunday School Quarterly will furnish a lifetime study guide for Bible study. The suggested passages in the Quarterly go through the entire Bible using an excellent system. Specialized studies may be done by studying one book at a time or key words, subjects, or characters of the Bible.

5. *Study regularly.*

Every day study a few verses from the suggested passage. It is better to study briefly each day than for a long period on just one day in the week (Acts 17:11).

6. *Write down your study.*

Capture each study permanently by writing our thoughts on paper. It is a proven study method. Use it and be amazed at the increased learning ability this method will produce. It is strongly suggested that you keep a notebook in which you can keep your studies. (Suggested methods are given at the end of this chapter)

7. *Apply to life and share with others.*

The Bible is learned when it is lived. Translate the truths and principles of God's word into daily living.

Share each study with others. Share God's word with the lost by witnessing to them of the living Christ of the scripture. Share it with Christian friends as you fellowship in homes, Sunday School classes, etc.

APPROACHES TO BIBLE STUDY

* Reading for refreshment
  * Memorizing key verses
    * Search the Scripture methods

1. *READING FOR REFRESHMENT* in leisure time without limiting the number of verses to be read. It will probably astonish many to know that one single issue of some of our national magazines contains as much reading matter as the entire New Testament. Thousands read these magazines through every week. Yet very few Christians read through the New Testament every week, or even one whole book of the New Testament.

A suggested plan would be to read four chapters a day from four key sections of the Bible. Start the first day with Genesis, Chapter 1; 1 Chronicles, Chapter 1; Psalm, Chapter 1; and Matthew, Chapter 1. Second day, read Genesis 2, 1 Chronicles 2, Psalm 2, and Matthew 2, and on and on through the sections.

Each of these divisions deals with the beginning of things, (except the Psalms) and covers the entire story of God's dealings with man. The Psalms is a book of praise. As you finish a section start over in that same section. Therefore, you will always be reading praise from the Psalms, always reading from the New Testament, and from two sections of the Old Testament.

As you read, discipline yourself to write down the key words, key phrases, and the key ideas of each chapter. Keep them in a notebook and at the end of the year you will have summarized every chapter in the Bible in a few statements. This personal commentary of thoughts could become invaluable.

2. *MEMORIZING KEY VERSES*

(1) *WHY MEMORIZE SCRIPTURE?*

Because of God's command.

"And these words, which I command thee this day, shall be in thine heart" (Deut. 6:6).

"Write them upon the table of thine heart: so shalt thou find favour and good understanding in the sight of God and man" (Prov. 3:3,4).

Because it enables us to meditate upon God's word anytime, anywhere.

"But his delight is in the law of the Lord; and in his law doth he meditate day and night" (Psalm 1:2).

"This book of the law shall not depart out of thy mouth; but thou shalt meditate therein day and night, that thou mayest observe to do according to all that is written therein: for then thou shalt make thy way prosperous, and then thou shalt have good success" (Joshua 1:8).

Because it gives victory over sin and Satan.

"Thy word have I hid in mine heart, that I might not sin against thee" (Ps. 119:11).

Because it makes your witnessing more effective.

(a) Fills the heart with what to say (Jer. 20:9). (b) Permits us to speak with confidence: "So shall I have wherewith to answer him that reproacheth me: for I trust in thy word" (Ps. 119:42). (c) Enables us to always be ready (I Peter 3:15). "Have not I written to thee excellent things in counsels and knowledge, that I might make thee know the certainty of the words of truth; that thou mightest answer the words of truth to them that send unto thee" (Prov. 22:20,21). (d) Because it allows the Holy Spirit to call verses to your remembrance for use in times of need. "But the Comforter, which is the Holy Ghost . . . shall teach you all things, and bring all things to your remembrance"

(John 14:26).

Every thought that goes into the mind is permanently recorded in the subconscious. Therefore, we need to fill it with the truth of God's Word so that the Holy Spirit can have these great truths to use as His Sword in giving victory over sin and Satan. Filling our mind with the things of the world and not the truth of God will bring sure defeat.

Billy Graham has said "I believe that regular, systematic memorization of Scripture is one of the most effective means of growth for a Christian. I recommend it to pastors, businessmen, professional people, everyone, as a rich source of blessing for their lives."

(2) *HOW TO MEMORIZE SCRIPTURE:*

Realize Scripture Memory is possible. Most people think they have poor memories. Yet the truth is that most have never developed their memories. It is a fact that most people only use one-tenth of their mental capacity. The old as well as the young can memorize. Some say, "I don't have time." Scripture memory doesn't take time; it saves time.

Have a simple plan. Learn so many each week. Don't try to learn too many as this can discourage and defeat the purpose of Scripture memory. A suggestion is one or two verses each week. Memorizing the Golden Text of the Sunday School lesson would be an excellent plan.

Apply the rules of memory.

(a) *Use the law of association.*

Associate the verse with a subject such as prayer, faith, etc.

(b) *Use the law of concentration.*

Don't be afraid to be still and THINK. Give the verse a second and third thought. It takes time to think through some subjects. Don't day-dream or rummage through waste thoughts. Get alone with God's thoughts. Don't concentrate upon yourself but dwell on Him.

"My soul shall be satisfied as with marrow and fatness; and my mouth shall praise Thee with joyful lips: When I remember Thee upon my bed, and meditate on Thee in the night watches" (Ps. 63:5,6).

(c) *Use the law of understanding.*

Know what the verse is about. We haven't memorized when we can simply quote the words. We must understand what we memorize if it is to become a part of us and become usable in our walk with Christ.

(d) *Use the law of review.*

Review each day. Review the more difficult verses more often. The secret of learning is review, review, review.

D. *Trust the Holy Spirit to bring verses to your mind when they are needed in your walk with Christ.*

"But the Comforter (Counselor, Helper, Intercessor, Advocate, Strengthener, Standby), the Holy Spirit, Whom the Father will send in My name (in My place, to represent Me and act on My behalf) He will teach you all things. And He will cause you to recall—will remind you of, bring to your remembrance—everything I have told you" (John 14:26).

AVAILABLE MEMORY COURSES

Topical Memory System, a 108 verse correspondence course in six steps, streamlined for busy people. Individual enrolment necessary from: The Navigators, Colorado Springs, Colorado.

Youth, children through adults, *Memory Course* can be gotten from Bible Memory Association, P.O. Box 12,000, St. Louis, Missouri, 63112. A small enrollment fee is charged for each of these series.

3. *SEARCHING THE SCRIPTURES—A SIMPLE METHOD OF SEARCHING THE SCRIPTURES:*

A SEARCH THE SCRIPTURE STUDY may be done on the entire passage, or a single verse. What you do depends on the time you have. Suggested passages in your Sunday School Lesson Quarterly offer an excellent system of going through the Bible.

First, PARAPHRASE THE PASSAGE—"What does it say?" Read through the passage carefully. Look for key words, key phrases, and key ideas.

To do a SUMMARY, briefly rewrite the passage in your own words including all the important thoughts. This is done by putting the thoughts of the passage into your own personal language. Rewrite the passage as if you were telling it to a friend.

To do an *OUTLINE,* divide the passage into its natural thoughts on paragraphs. Some Bibles do this for you. Give a brief title to each

thought, such as "The Way to Pray." Use subpoints as you find the
need.

EXAMPLE:
Title: PRAYER WHICH BRINGS REWARD
Matt. 6:5–15

I. The wrong way to pray 6:5–8
   1. Do not pray to be seen of men 6:5,6
   2. Do not pray to be heard of men 6:7,8
II. The right way to pray 6:9–15
   1. Pray to the Father with deep respect 6:9
   2. Pray that God's will be done 6:10
   3. Pray for your daily needs 6:11
   4. Pray for forgiveness 6:12
   5. Pray to be delivered from evil 6:13
   6. Pray for willingness to forgive others 6:14,15

Second, the PROBLEMS OF THE PASSAGE—"What does it say that
I do not understand?" Write down the things you do not fully understand,
then, indicate which verse or verses. Do not list a reference and simply add,
"I do not understand." Explain what you don't understand. It may be a word,
or an idea.

Last, the PROFIT OF THE PASSAGE—"What does it say to me?" In
writing this most valuable part of the study use the personal pronouns "I"
and "me."

You may find these suggestions helpful:

(1) State the truth of the passage briefly in your own words. This may be
drawn from one verse or several. Indicate how this applies to you. Ask
questions: "What need does this bring out in my life? What new appreciation
or understanding does it give? What does God want me to do?" Ask yourself
key questions.

1. What is the subject of this Chapter?
2. What is the leading lesson of this Chapter?
3. Which is the best verse in this Chapter?
4. Who are the principle persons of this Chapter?
5. What does the Chapter teach concerning Christ?
6. Is there any example for me to follow?
7. Is there any error for me to avoid?
8. Is there any duty for me to perform?

9. Is there any promise for me to claim?

10. Is there any prayer for me to echo?

(2) Write what you intend to do about it NOW . . . to correct the weakness, build a needed quality into the life, strengthen the understanding, etc. Sometimes this action may be obeying a command, making a special study of the subject, memorizing a key verse, or praying about the need. It may be writing a letter of apology, righting some wrong done or doing some kindness. Be specific and check back to see if you have followed through.

Chapter 8

HOW TO START
A PRAYER TIME

Christ's life was filled with prayer. "Very early the next morning, long before daylight, Jesus got up and left the house. He went out of town to a lonely place where he prayed" (Mark 1:35, TEV). If you want to grow and be like him you need to spend time with him each day in prayer.

Jesus said, "They ought always to pray and not to turn coward —faint, lose heart and give up" (Luke 18:1). He indicated that if we do not pray, we will faint. If we are to walk victoriously in Christ, we must take time to pray.

At first, it may be hard to pray. But even those who first followed Jesus had to learn how. They went to Jesus and said, "Lord, teach us to pray" (Luke 11:1).

I. WHY HAVE A PRAYER TIME?

1. Prayer played a most important part in the daily life of Jesus. "And in the morning, long before daylight, He got up and went out to a deserted place, and there He prayed" (Mark 1:35).

2. The apostles regarded prayer as the most important business of their lives.

"But we will continue to devote ourselves steadfastly to prayer and the ministry of the Word" (Acts 6:4).

3. It is God's way for us to obtain His blessings.

"Do not fret or have any anxiety about anything, but in every circumstance and in everything by prayer and petition (definite requests) with thanksgiving continue to make your wants known to God" (Phil. 4:6).

"Up to this time, you have not asked a (single) thing in My name (that is, presenting all I AM) (but now) ask and keep on asking and you will receive, so that your joy (gladness, delight) may be full and complete" (John 16:24).

4. Through prayer we have personal fellowship with God and His Son, Jesus.

"And (this) fellowship that we have (which is a distinguishing mark of Christians) is with the Father and with His Son Jesus Christ, the Messiah" (I John 1:3).

5. Prayer gives power to overcome sin and Satan.

"Let us then fearlessly and confidently and boldly draw near to the throne of grace—the throne of God's unmerited favor (to us sinners); that we may receive mercy (for our failures) and find grace to help in good time for every need—appropriate help and well-timed help, coming just when we need it" (Heb. 4:16).

6. Prayer aids in witnessing.

"Brethren, (with all) my heart's desire and goodwill for (Israel) I long and pray to God that they may be saved" (Rom. 10:1).

II. How to Have a Daily Prayer Time?

* DEFINITE PERIOD OF TIME
* DEFINITE PLACE OF QUIET
* SIMPLE PLAN OF PROCEDURE

1. *Set a Definite Period of Time*

"Now when Daniel knew that the writing was signed, he went into his house; and his windows being open in his chamber, toward Jerusalem, he kneeled upon his knees three times a day, and prayed, and gave thanks before his God, as he did aforetime. Then these men assembled, and found Daniel praying and making supplication before his God" (Daniel 6:10,11).

(1) Daily. Daniel prayed three times a DAY. You may not be able to pray three times, but you should be able to pray at least one time daily. Set aside a time each day to fellowship with your Lord Jesus.

"Evening, and morning, and at noon, will I pray, and cry aloud;

and he shall hear my voice" (Psalm 55:17).

(2) Early morning, if possible. This is the Bible's ideal.

"My voice shalt thou hear in the morning, O Lord; in the morning will I direct my prayer unto thee; and will look up" (Psalm 5:3).

"Cause me to hear thy lovingkindness in the morning; for in thee do I trust: cause me to know the way wherein I would walk; for I lift up my soul unto thee" (Psalm 143:8).

How do you get up early? Going to bed at night is a step in the right direction!

(3) Begin with a time schedule you can and will keep—Suggest you start with 7–10 minutes DAILY.

2. *Have a Definite Place of Quiet.*

(1) Completely alone. Daniel went into his house. Jesus went into the hills and mountains.

"And after He had dismissed the multitude. He went up into the hills by Himself to pray. When it was evening He was still there alone" (Matt. 14:23).

(2) Away from noise and distractions. "But when you pray, go into your most private room, and closing the door, pray to your Father Who is in secret; and your Father Who sees in secret will reward you in the open" (Matt. 6:6).

Let this become a holy (set apart) place.

3. *Use a Simple Plan of Procedure.*

Plan ahead what you will do so you will not waste time.

(1) Prepare the heart—"Be still and know that I am God" (Psalm 46:10). Samuel Chadwick said, "Hurry is the death of prayer."

Pray that your heart may be open to His voice. "Open thou mine eyes, that I may behold wondrous things out of the law" (Psalm 119:18).

(2) Partake of His Word.

"I have esteemed the words of his mouth more than my necessary food" (Job 23:12b).

a. Have a definite plan of going through the Bible. Decide on a method you will use—Sunday School Bible readings or a book of the Bible through: a few verses or a chapter at a time. A suggestion for reading through the Bible in a year is shared in Chapter 7.

b. Read carefully, expectantly.
   (a) Meditate on the passage—concentrate.
   (b) Look for truth that meets your need.
   (c) Let God speak to you personally. Your greatest need is to hear a word from God.
c. Take notes. Write down thoughts which God gives you as you read.

(3) Pray intelligently and purposefully. After God has spoken to you through His Word, then speak to Him in prayer. You can easily develop a pattern of prayer using the word A C T S as a guide.

A—*Adoration*—Begin by entering into fellowship with God with great respect and admiration. You wouldn't barge into the presence of the President. You would begin with the proper salutation: so with God. Worship Him. Tell the Lord you love Him. Reflect on His greatness—His power—His mercy—His patience—His majesty and sovereignty. Look in the Psalms for help. "Praise ye the Lord. Praise God in his Sanctuary: praise him in the firmament of his power. Praise him for his mighty acts: praise him according to his excellent greatness" (Psalm 150:1,2).

C—*Confession follows*—As you come into God's presence you will be convicted of your sins. Now you will want to confess every known sin and be sure it is cleansed and forsaken. Confession comes from a word meaning, "to agree together with." Apply this to prayer. It means to agree with God's viewpoint. Something happened yesterday, and I called it a slight exaggeration: God calls it a lie! I call it strong language: God calls it swearing! I call it telling the truth about somebody in church: God calls it gossip! I call it human nature: God calls it lust of the flesh! "If I regard iniquity (sin) in my heart the Lord will not hear me" (Psalm 66:18). But if we confess, God forgives. "If we (freely) admit that we have sinned and confess our sins, He is faithful and just (true to His own nature and promises) and will forgive our sins (dismiss our lawlessness) and continuously cleanse us from all unrighteousness" (1 John 1:9).

T—*Thanksgiving*—Think of several specific things to thank God for—your salvation, your family, friends, health, life, job, your church and its ministry. Thank Him for even tight places. "Thank

(God) in everything—no matter what the circumstances may be, be thankful and give thinks; for this is the will of God for you (who are) in Christ Jesus (the Revealer and Mediator of that will)" (1 Thess. 5:18). (Psalm 118:1; Phil. 4:5).

S—*Supplication*—Means "to ask for, earnestly and humbly." This is the part of your prayer in which you make your requests known to God. Pray first for others—friends, unsaved, missionaries, the sick, then pray for your own needs. "Confess to one another therefore your faults—your slips, your false steps, your offenses, your sins; and pray (also) for one another, that you may be healed and restored—to a spiritual tone of mind and heart. The earnest (heartfelt, continued) prayer of a righteous man makes tremendous power available" (James 5:16). "Bear (endure, carry) one another's burdens and troublesome moral faults, and in this way fulfill and observe perfectly the law of Christ" (Gal. 6:2). "Pray at all times—on every occasion, in every season—in the Spirit, with all (manner of) prayer and entreaty. To that end keep alert and watch with strong purpose and perseverance, interceding in behalf of all the saints" (Eph. 6:18).

Example of One Day's Prayer Time in 10 Minutes

60 seconds—Prepare the heart (open your Bible, clear your mind)
5 minutes—Partake of the Word (Read the Bible—Let God speak)
4 minutes—Pray—*A*—Adore God; *C*—Confess all known sin;
 T—Thank Him; *S*—Supplication for others—for your needs.

GUARD YOUR PRAYER TIME

Satan will use every device to cause you to miss one day, and when you do—BEWARE! Defeat is near!

Chapter 9

HOW TO
GET INVOLVED
IN THE CHURCH

Jesus Christ personally established the church while He was here on the earth to unite Christians together as a spiritual family of God (Matt. 16:18; 28:19).

Just as we are physically born into our earthly families, Jesus said we must be born again, or be spiritually born into God's family (John 3:3).

God has placed men in families for their care, protection, fellowship and development; and we need the church for all the reasons we need a family and many more.

The church is God's plan for uniting Christians together to worship Him and carry on His great works. It is one of God's ways of strengthening the believer in his Christian walk.

Every Christian must belong to, and faithfully attend, and serve in a church if he is to walk victoriously in Christ.

I. WHAT IS A NEW TESTAMENT CHURCH?

A church is a spiritual family, a fellowship of baptized believers voluntarily joining themselves together for worship and study to carry out the commands of Christ. It is a "colony of heaven" placed here in a foreign land to show this world of darkness the grace of God's eternal salvation.

1. It is a saved fellowship

"And the Lord kept adding (to their number) daily those who were being saved (from spiritual death)" (Acts 2:47).

2. It is a love fellowship

"By this shall all (men) know that you are My disciples, if you love one another" (John 13:35).

3. It is a worshipping fellowship

"You shall worship the Lord your God and Him alone shall you serve" (Matt. 4:10).

"And day after day they regularly assembled in the temple with united purpose, and in their homes they broke bread (including the Lord's Supper). They partook of their food with gladness and simplicity and generous hearts, constantly praising God and being in favor and goodwill with all the people" (Acts 2:46,47).

4. It is a witnessing fellowship

"But you shall receive power—ability, efficiency and might—when the Holy Spirit has come upon you; and you shall be My witnesses in Jerusalem and all Judea and Samaria and to the ends—the very bounds of the earth" (Acts 1:8).

5. It is a discipling fellowship

"Therefore put away from among yourselves that wicked person" (1 Cor. 5:13; 1 Cor. 5:1–13).

"Admonish (warn and seriously advise) those who are out of line— the loafers, the disorderly and the unruly" (1 Thess. 5:14).

II. WHAT IS THE MAIN MISSION OF THIS
FELLOWSHIP OF BELIEVERS?

* TO WITNESS TO THE LOST
* TO BUILD UP THE SAVED

"Go then and make disciples of all the nations, baptizing them into the name of the Father and of the Son and of the Holy Spirit; teaching them to observe everything that I have commanded you, and lo, I am with you all the days,—perpetually, uniformly and on every occasion—to the very close and consummation of the age" (Matt. 28: 19–20).

1. *To witness to the lost*

"You shall be My witnesses . . . to the ends—the very bounds—of the earth" (Acts 1:8).

"And He said to them, Go into all the world and preach and

publish openly the good news (the Gospel) to every creature (of the whole human race)" (Mark 16:15).

"When He saw the throngs, He was moved with pity and sympathy for them, because they were bewildered—harassed and distressed and dejected and helpless—like sheep without a shepherd (Zech. 10:2). Then He said to His disciples, the harvest is indeed plentiful" (Matt. 9:36,37).

"Do you not say, "It is still four months until harvest time comes? Look! I tell you, raise your eyes and observe the fields and see how they are already white for harvesting" (John 4:35).

2. *To Build up the saved in the faith*

"And His gifts were (varied; He Himself appointed and gave men to us,) some to be apostles (special messengers), some prophets (inspired preachers and expounders), some evangelists (preachers of the Gospel, traveling missionaries), some pastors (shepherds of His flock) and teachers: His intention was the perfecting and the full equipping of the saints (His consecrated people), (that they should do) the work of ministering toward building up Christ's body (the church) that (we might arrive) at really mature manhood, the measure of the stature of the fullness of the Christ: So then, we may no longer be children, tossed (like ships) to and from between chance gusts of teaching, and wavering with every changing wind of doctrine, (the prey of) the cunning and cleverness of unscrupulous men, (gamblers engaged) in every shifting form of trickery in inventing errors to mislead; rather, let our lives lovingly express truth in all things—speaking truly, dealing truly, living truly. Enfolded in love, let us grow up in every way and in all things into Him, Who is the Head, (even) Christ, the Messiah, the Anointed One" (Eph. 4:11–15).

III. WHAT RESPONSIBILITIES DOES EACH CHRISTIAN HAVE TO THE FELLOWSHIP OF BELIEVERS?

1. *To Pray*

"Confess to one another therefore your faults; and pray (also) for one another" (James 5:16).

"Pray at all times—on every occasion, in every season—in the Spirit, with all (manner of) prayer and entreaty. To that end keep alert and watch with strong purpose and perseverance, interceding in behalf of all the saints" (Eph. 6:18).

"So Peter was kept in prison; but fervent prayer for him was persistently made to God by the church" (Acts 12:5).

2. *To Attend*

"So let us seize and hold fast and retain without wavering the hope we cherish and confess; (for He Who promised is reliable and faithful) and let us consider and give attentive, continuous care to watching over one another to love and helpful deeds and noble activities; not forsaking or neglecting to assemble together (as believers), as is the habit of some people, but admonishing one another, and all the more faithfully as you see the day approaching" (Heb. 10:23–25).

3. *To Support*

"Let each one (give) as he has made up his own mind and purposed in his heart, not reluctantly or sorrowfully or under compulsion, for God loves a cheerful giver" (2 Cor. 9:7).

"But if anyone has this world's goods and sees his brother and fellow believer in need, yet closes his heart of compassion against him, how can the love of God live and remain in him" (1 John 3:17).

"Now concerning the money contributed for the saints; you are to do the same as I directed the churches of Galatia to do. One the first (day) of each week, let everyone of you (personally) put aside something and save it up as he has prospered" (1 Cor. 16:1,2).

4. *To Serve*

"As each of you has received a gift, employ it for one another as good trustees of God's many-sided grace. Whoever speaks oracles of God; whoever renders service, (let him do it) as with the strength which God furnishes abundantly; so that in all things God may be glorified through Jesus Christ. To Him be the glory and dominion for ever and ever" (1 Peter 4:10,11) (1 Cor. 12:1–31).

5. *To Keep Unity*

"Fill up and complete my joy by living in harmony and being of the same mind and one in purpose, having the same love, being in full accord and of one harmonious mind. Do nothing from strife or conceit; let each regard the others as better than yourselves. Look not upon his own interests, but also each for the interest of others. Let this same attitude and purpose and mind be in you which was in Christ Jesus" (Phil. 2:2–5).

"God hateth . . . (him) that soweth discord among the brethren" (Prob. 6:16,19).

"I appeal to you, brethren, to be on your guard concerning those who create dissensions and difficulties and cause divisions, in opposition to the doctrine which you have been taught; avoid them. For such persons do not serve our Lord Christ but their own appetites and base desires, and by ingratiating and flattering speech they beguile the hearts of the unsuspecting and simple-minded (people)" (Rom. 16: 17,18).

6. *To Encourage each other*

"Bear (endure, carry) on another's burdens, and in this way fulfill the law of Christ" (Gal. 6:2).

"Practice hospitality to one another and do it ungrudgingly" (1 Peter 4:9).

7. *To Respect and follow it's leaders*

"Now also we beseech you, brethren, get to know those who labor among you, your leaders who are over you in the Lord, and those who warn and kindly reprove and exhort you; and hold them in very high esteem in appreciation of their work" (1 Thess. 5:12,13).

"Obey your spiritual leaders and submit to them; for they are constantly keeping watch over your souls, as men who will have to render an account, let them do this with gladness, and not with sighing and groaning, for that would not be profitable to you" (Heb. 13:17).

Chapter 10

HOW TO
SHARE CHRIST
WITH OTHERS

Our Lord's last parting request and command was, "You shall be My witnesses" (Acts 1:8). R. A. Torrey once said, "The only real reason God has left us here on this earth is to point other men to Jesus." Witnessing is every Christian's privilege and responsibility.

Christians, arise! Christ has commanded us to evangelize the world! He has commissioned us to take the gospel message of salvation to every person in the uttermost parts of the earth. This is to be done in every generation. The Lord has made us responsible today for the people of today.

In the New Testament day there was no radio, television, or printed page to aid in evangelism. Yet it was said of the Christians in Rome that their faith was "spoken of throughout the whole world" (Rom. 1:8); and of the Thessalonians," the Word from the Lord resounded forth from you . . . everywhere" (1 Thess. 1:8).

What had made this mighty impact upon the rest of the world? It was the TRANSFORMED LIVES OF THESE CHRISTIANS who went about telling what Christ had done for them. These men had been with Jesus and the world took notice of the great difference it made in their lives (Acts 4:13).

Personal witnessing is the only way this world will ever hear the message of Christ. Only a small per cent of the lost ever attend church. That means that most of the lost population have little or no concern for religion. Many unsaved will never be saved unless someone goes into their homes and leads them to know Christ. If they do not come to us, we must go to them.

Paul told the Ephesian Church in Acts 20:20, "How I did not shrink from telling you anything that was for your benefit, and teaching you in public meetings and from HOUSE TO HOUSE." New Testament evangelism has two approaches which are dependent upon each other: pulpit evanglism and personal evangelism. Someone has said that for every reference to pulpit evangelism, there are nine to personal evangelism. Billy Graham has said, "Strange as it may seem, I get a far greater thrill out of leading one person in my room to Christ than I do out of one meeting where I see hundreds come."

WHAT IS CHRISTIAN WITNESSING?

A witness is one who tells what he has seen and heard, what he has experienced. He does not argue or he would become a lawyer. Many have felt that Christian witnessing is like being a good salesman, or a powerful lawyer. A witness is used by the lawyer, and often the case is won or lost because of the effectiveness of the witness; but a witness is not a lawyer. God has not called us to be lawyers, judges, or even salesmen, but He has called us to be WITNESSES. The Holy Spirit is the spiritual advocate, or lawyer, who convicts the sinner of his sins, and we are to be His witnesses.

The word "witness" comes from the Greek word, *martus*, which means "martyr." It signifies that one not only talks with his lips, but he is willing to pay for the privilege of doing it with his blood (Phil. 1:29). He is not seeking to please and satisfy. He will not care what others think of him if they wish to criticize and scoff. He is only concerned about what God thinks. "But just as we have been approved by God to be entrusted with the glad tidings (the Gospel), so we speak not to please men, but to please God, Who tests our hearts" (1 Thess. 2:4).

ESSENTIALS TO EFFECTIVE WITNESSING

1. *DEPENDENCE UPON THE HOLY SPIRIT*

As Christian witnesses we must rely upon the Holy Spirit to bring conviction to the lost. One of the great dangers in witnessing is to try to bring the lost under conviction with our arguments and persuasion.

We must remember that we are witnesses; the Holy Spirit must convict (John 16:8–11). We are to present Christ. Jesus said, "No one comes to the Father except by (through) Me" (John 14:6).

2. *A DEDICATED WALK IN CHRIST*

After Paul had been converted, he received instruction from Ananias, a devout Christian, which aptly summarizes the Christian's walk and work (Acts 2:14,15).

Paul was, first, to get to know God's will. This was to be done through the personal experience of looking at and listening to Jesus. It was then that he was to witness to others what he had seen and heard.

To be an effective witness we must know the heart of God. This must be the supreme objective of every believer. In order to know the will of God, we must take time to get to know Christ. We must see Him as He shows Himself to us through the living Word of God and as He lives within us. It is then that we can witness to others what we have seen and heard. It is only after we have taken time to walk in Christ that we have something to witness to others. Someone has said, "Witnessing is getting a good look at Jesus and then telling another what you have seen and heard."

When Jesus called his first disciples, He said, "Come after Me—letting Me be your Guide, follow Me—and I will make you fishers of men" (Matt. 4:19). The basic principles involved within this verse will give further understanding of the pattern for our becoming a fruitful, witnessing Christian in carrying out the desire of our Lord to evangelize the world. The command of Christ is for us to follow Him. The promise is that when we do, He will make us fishers of men. We cannot follow Christ without fishing for men; we cannot fish for men unless we are following Christ. If we are walking in Christ, we will witness; if we are not witnessing, there is something wrong with our walk.

The foremost question each of us must ask, "Am I following the Lord Jesus? Am I walking daily with Him?"

USE YOUR PERSONAL TESTIMONY

The personal testimony is at the heart of Christian witnessing.

Throughout the book of Acts, Paul made much use of his personal testimony. He told about his life before he was converted; how he felt when the Lord spoke to him and how he called upon the Lord to come into his life; and how the Lord affected his life from that moment on. Paul always magnified the Lord Jesus Christ. He said, "For me, to live is Christ—His life in me; and to die is gain—(the gain of the glory of eternity)" (Phil. 1:21).

Many people do not feel that their testimony is interesting enough to tell. Yet anyone who has come to know Christ has something to share with others that is vitally interesting.

One of the problems is that most have never clearly thought through their testimony, or formulated it in a way in which it could be told easily. One of the best ways to do this is to WRITE OUT YOUR TESTIMONY (1) giving adequate details, (2) and using words which would be understood by a person not familiar with church talk. For example, instead of only using the word "convicted" explain the word by telling how you felt when you were convicted. Write out your testimony, and then rewrite it, leaving out points which do not seem essential and adding facts which will come to your mind which seem more important. Writing out your testimony several times will prove extremely helpful in clearly formulating your experience.

Suggestions for Writing Out Your Testimony

1. Tell about your life before you were saved: where you were born—where you grew up—where you attended school. Relate any time you felt convicted and impressed that you ought to become a Christian. Tell what hindered you most from becoming a Christian. (Those who were converted at an early age will not have as much to share from this point as others. Of course, they should rejoice that they found Christ so early in life.)

2. Describe your experience of accepting Christ. Was it in revival, regular service, or elsewhere? If someone helped you to know how to pray, relate this. Write down what you asked the Lord to do for you.

3. How has Christ affected your life since you have been saved—at home, at work, or school; through problems and difficulties; attitudes toward others; desires; feelings for the lost?

Suggestions for Using Your Testimony

1. Share your testimony with lost friends by weaving basic Scripture verses into your experiences with the Lord. An example would be: "Bill, here in Romans 3:23 God says that ALL have sinned. I remember when I realized that my life was lived for self. I knew I wasn't giving God any place in my life. I came to know that I was included in 'ALL HAVE SINNED.'"

2. Share your testimony with Christian friends. Emphasize what has helped you the most in your Christian life to grow and develop spiritually. Point out how Bible study, prayer, church attendance, etc., have helped you. Many have testified that through the testimony of Christian friends they have learned how to overcome problems in their lives, how to study the Bible more effectively; what they needed to do to grow spiritually, etc.

USING A NEW TESTAMENT

God has promised to honor His word, not our arguments. It is the instrument God uses to convict of sin and to reveal Christ to the unsaved. "For the Word that God speaks is alive and full of power—making it active, operative, energizing and effective; it is sharper than any two-edged sword, penetrating to the dividing line of the breath of life (soul) and (the immortal) spirit, and of joints and marrow (that is, of the deepest parts of our nature) exposing and sifting and analyzing and judging the very thoughts and purposes of the heart" (Heb. 4:12).

"The sword the Spirit wields, which is the Word of God" (Eph. 6:17). If we have a working knowledge of some basic verses, the Holy Spirit will be able to make us more effective witnesses.

PRACTICAL SUGGESTIONS

1. Carry a small New Testament which may be concealed in the pocket or purse. This will enable you to be ready at the proper moment to reach for it and use if for the glory of the Lord.

2. Mark or underline the basic verses if you feel this will help you to be more effective.

3. Use it! Don't defend it! It is the Word of God whether the unsaved believes it or not. It alone points to the way of salvation.

BASIC PASSAGES

1. *SETS OF VERSES*
Discover the verses which you are able to use easily and naturally, and master them.

(1) Verses from ROMANS
Romans 3:23—"Since all have sinned and are falling short of the honor and glory which God bestows and receives."

Romans 5:8—"But God shows and clearly proves His (own) love for us by the fact that while we were still sinners Christ, the Messiah, the Anointed One, died for us."

Romans 6:23—"For the wages which sin pays is death; but the (bountiful) free gift of God is eternal life through Jesus Christ our Lord."

Romans 10:9,10—"Because if you acknowledge and confess with your lips that Jesus is Lord and in your heart believe that God raised Him from the dead, you will be saved. For with the heart a person believes and so is justified (declared righteous, acceptable to God), and with the mouth he confesses and confirms (his) salvation."

Romans 10:13—"For every one who calls upon the name of the Lord will be saved." Joel 2:32.

(2) Verses from JOHN:
John 1:1—"In the beginning (before all time) was the Word (Christ), and the Word was with God, and the Word was God Himself." (Isa. 9:6) (Who Christ is).

John 1:14—"And the Word (Christ) became flesh (human, incarnate) and tabernacled—fixed His tent of flesh, lived awhile—among us; and we (actually) saw His glory—His honor, His majesty; such glory as an only begotten son receives from his father, full of grace (favor, loving kindness) and truth." (Isa. 40:5) (What Christ became).

John 3:3—"Jesus answered him, I assure you, most solemnly I tell you, that unless a person is born again (anew, from above), he cannot ever see—know, be acquainted with (and experience)—the kingdom of God." (What man needs.)

John 3:16—"For God so greatly loved and dearly prized the world that He (even) gave up His only begotten Son, so that whoever believes in (trusts, clings to, relies on) Him may not perish—come to destruction, be lost—but have eternal (everlasting) life." (Who God provided for man's need.)

John 3:36—"And he who believes on—has faith in, clings to, relies on—the Son has (now possesses) eternal life. But whoever disobeys—is unbelieving toward, refuses to trust in, disregards, is not subject to—the Son will never see (experience) life. But instead the wrath of God abides on him." Hab. 2:4. (What man must do.)

    (3) *A B C PLAN*

A.—All have sinned—Romans 3:23, 6:23

B.—Believe on Christ—John 8:16, 1:12; Acts 16:30, 31

C.—Confess sins and

    Call upon Christ—Romans 10:9,10,13

2. SOUL-WINNING INTERVIEWS OF JESUS

Many are finding that using only one passage of Scripture is less confusing than turning from book to book. The following passages point out (1) man's great need and (2) God's provision.

(1) Luke 18:18–30—Rich Man

This passage points out that not even the Lord Jesus successfully won everyone with whom He dealt. The rich young ruler loved money more than he loved Christ, and this kept him from being born again. But it also reveals that, with God's power, anyone can be saved.

(2) John 4:6–29—Woman at Well

(3) John 3:1–16—Religious Leader

(4) John 8:1–11—Sinful Woman

(5) Luke 19:1–19—Dishonest Business Man

(6) John 12:20–50—Certain Greeks

Using Your Testimony with Scriptures

Here is an illustration of a typical way to use the scriptures as you tell what Christ has done for you personally. This should be done after using a basic-approach technique which will prepare the unsaved for your witness.

WITNESS: "Bill, God says here in Romans 3:23 that ALL have sinned and come short of the glory of God. I remember when I realized that my life was lived for self. I knew I wasn't giving God a place in my life. I came to know that I was included in 'ALL HAVE SINNED.' Don't you feel, as I, that you have sinned?" (Point to the verse and allow his eyes to see it also.)

WITNESS: "Now, Bill, over in Romans 6:23 we find that the result of sin is death, separation from God. I suppose all of us have thought about what this means. I remember when I came to realize that there was no hope at all apart from this experience called salvation. It was then that I realized if I was to ever know any real happiness in my life, I had to call upon Jesus to take care of my sins.

"NOW LOOK at the last part of this verse, Bill: '. . . the gift of God is eternal life through Jesus Christ our Lord.' I'll never forget when I began to realize that God really loved me, personally. I had always throught of God's loving everybody in such a general way. But I realized He loved me!

WITNESS: "Let me read another verse of Scripture in Romans 5:8, 'But God shows and clearly proves His (own) love for us by the fact that while we were still sinners Christ, the Messiah, the Anointed One, died for us.' You see, Bill, even though you and I were sinners, God still loved us and sent Jesus to die for us on the cross.

WITNESS: "Bill, do you know John 3:16? I'm sure you have heard it read or quoted. 'For God so greatly loved and dearly prized the world that He (even) gave up His only begotten Son, so that whoever . . . 'believes in (trusts, clings to, relies on) Him may not perish—come to destruction, be lost—but have eternal (everlasting) life.' What does it say we have to do to have everlasting life?" (Pause briefly for an answer. If he doesn't answer soon, continue.)

"Now, I don't know about you, but I used to wonder just what that word 'believe' meant. I always thought I believed in Jesus before I ever became a Christian. I believed that He lived, and died, and even that He died on the cross for me. BUT I came to realize that to believe means so much more than that.

WITNESS: "Look at these verses in Romans 10:9,10: 'Because if you acknowledge and confess with you lips that Jesus is Lord and in your heart believe that God raised Him from the dead, you will be saved. For with the heart a person believes and so is justified (declared righteous, acceptable to God), and with the mouth he confesses and confirms (his) salvation.'

"In other words, Bill, you must believe with your heart as well as your head. You must trust yourself to Him as a real person, not just an idea. I remember the year————when I called upon the Lord to come into my life. I realized that being saved was more than knowing about Jesus: it was personally having Him come into my life because I asked Him to come in.

WITNESS: "Bill, I didn't know how to ask the Lord to come into my life, and maybe you are like I was. Let's turn to one other verse if you don't mind because it tells us how to call upon the Lord. In Revelation 3:20 the Lord Jesus says, 'Behold, I stand at the door and knock; if anyone hears and listens to and heeds My voice and opens the door, I will come in to him, and will eat with him, and he (shall eat) with Me.' This verse says that Jesus lets me know He wants to come into my life. HE SPEAKS AND HE KNOCKS TO GET IN. But it also tells me that I have to open the door of my heart, listen to Him as He speaks, and then invite Him to come into my heart. THIS IS THE MOST IMPORTANT DECISION I HAVE EVER MADE, BILL. And you can make it also.

"A while ago, we knocked on your door, and you opened it and invited us in. We wouldn't have come in if you hadn't asked us in. Now, Bill, Jesus loves you, He died for you, but He will not force His way into your life. He must be invited.

"If Christ is knocking on your heart right now, I pray you will open it to Him and ask Him to come in.

WITNESS: "Bill, let's have prayer." (Pray a simple prayer that the Holy Spirit will speak to this dear man's heart and that he will have the courage to ask the Lord Jesus to come into his life.)

WITNESS: "Now, Bill, ask the Lord to come into your heart and life." (Pause! Give him time to think. Don't force. If he hesitates very long, ask him if he knows what to pray. You may help him to know how and for what to pray. If he doesn't make his decision at this time, leave the door open for future visits.)

WITNESS: "Bill, let's thank the Lord for coming into your life." (Always have a prayer of thanksgiving when the person receives Christ. Take time to give him assurance by talking about this experience which he has just had. Talk with him about the importance of "following through" with baptism and church membership.)

WITNESS: "Now, if someone at work tomorrow asks you if you are a Christian, what will you say?"

Chapter 11

HOW TO
EXPERIENCE THE
SPIRIT-FILLED LIFE

When Jesus left this earth to return to the glories of Heaven, He did not leave us alone. He said, "and I will ask the Father, and He will give you another Comforter (Counselor, Helper, Intercessor, Advocate, Strengthener and Standby) that He may remain with you forever, the Spirit of Truth, whom the world cannot receive (welcome, take to its heart), because it does not see Him, nor know and recognize Him. But you know and recognize Him, for he lives with you (constantly) and will be in you. I will not leave you orphans—comfortless, desolate, bereaved, forlorn, helpless—*I will come (back) to you.* At that time—when that day comes—you will know (for yourselves) that I am in My Father, and you (are) in Me, and I (am) in you." (John 14:16–20).

He also said, "However, I am telling you nothing but the truth when I say, it is profitable—good expedient, advantageous—for you that I go away. Because if I do not go away, the Comforter (Counselor, Helper, Advocate, Intercessor, Strengthener, Standby) will not come to you—into close fellowship with you. But if I go away, I will send Him to you—to be in close fellowship with you. But when He, the Spirit of Truth (the truth-giving Spirit) comes, he will guide you into all the truth—the whole, full truth. For He will not speak His own message—on His own authority—but He will tell whatever He hears (from the Father). He will give the message that has been given to Him, and He will announce and declare to you the things that are to come—that will happen in the future" (John 16:7,13).

When you invited the Lord Jesus into your life, He actually and literally came to live in you. Christianity is LIFE—the life of Christ coming into you at the moment you are born again, and then living through your body each moment of each day. It is not imitating Christ; it is the indwelling of Christ. It is not trying to live like Christ; it is trusting Christ to live in and through you.

Paul said, "Christ liveth in me" (Gal. 2:20); and "Christ in you, the hope of glory" (Col. 1:27). He also said, "What? know ye not that your body is the temple of the Holy Spirit which is in you, which ye have of God, and ye are not your own? For ye are bought with a price: therefore glorify God in your body, and in your spirit, which are God's." (1 Cor. 6:19,20); and "Jesus Christ is in you" (2 Cor. 13:5).

God's Word conclusively testifies that when you are BORN AGAIN, the Lord Jesus, as the Holy Spirit, actually comes to live in your body.

Failure to realize that Christ lives in you will result in discouragement and defeat. If you think of Christ simply being near you, rather than living in you, your constant efforts will be to get closer to Him, or to get Him closer to you. However, the truth is Christ lives in you. Know this! Believe this! Experience this!

He is more than a helper to assist you; more than a teacher to instruct you; and more than a friend to encourage you. He does more than give you strength, He is your strength. He is life, your life—As Paul said, "I live; yet not I, but Christ liveth in me" (Gal. 2:20). "Without Him you can do nothing" (John 15:5).

A victorious Christian life is possible only as we deny ourselves and depend upon the Indwelling Christ, the Holy Spirit. And if we try to live our life directed by self, we shall lose it; but if we deny self and allow Christ to live His life fully within us, we shall gain the abundant life (Luke 9:23-25; Rom. 8:13).

Paul said, "For me, to live is Christ—His life in me; and to die is gain—the gain of the glory of eternity" (Phil. 1:21). "I have been crucified with Christ—(in Him) I have shared His crucifixion; it is no longer I who live, but Christ, the Messiah, lives in me; and the life I now live in the body I live by faith—by adherence to and reliance on and (complete) trust—in the Son of God, Who loved me and gave

Himself up for me" (Gal. 2:20).

Paul again said: "If we live by the (Holy) Spirit, let us also walk by the Spirit.—If by the (Holy) Spirit we have our life (in God), let us go forward walking in line, our conduct controlled by the Spirit" (Gal. 5:25). "But I say, walk and live habitually in the (Holy) Spirit—responsive to and controlled and guided by the Spirit; then you will certainly not gratify the cravings and desires of the flesh—of human nature with God" (Gal. 5:16). "And do not get drunk with wine, for that is debauchery; but ever be filled and stimulated with the (Holy) Spirit (Prov. 23:20)" (Eph. 5:18). To experience the Spirit-filled life you must be addicted to the controlling presence and power of the Holy Spirit who lives within.

I. WHO IS THE HOLY SPIRIT?

A common misconception is that He is an "it," or an influence, or a spiritual power. But the Holy Spirit is not any of these. He is a divine personality of the Godhead who has the characteristics of a person and performs actions that only a person could perform.

God has three personalities which are often referred to as the Trinity. The name "God" is used to mean all three persons of the Trinity; God the Father, God the Son, and God the Spirit. So, the Spirit is a divine PERSON, just as the Father and the Son are divine persons. And God in three persons has existed for all eternity.

You may better understand the Trinity if you think of a man who is a father, a son, and a husband: one man, yet three functions or manifestations of himself. God is one God, yet He has manifested Himself in three personalities.

"So there are three witnesses in heaven, the Father, the Word and the Holy Spirit, and these three are One; and there are three witnesses on the earth, the Spirit, the water, and the blood; and these three agree—are in unison, their testimony coincides" (1 John 5:8).

II. WHAT IS THE WORK OF THE HOLY SPIRIT?

The Holy Spirit was sent by the Father and the Son (John 16:7); to present Jesus (1) to the lost that they might be saved, and (2) to the saved that they might develop to witness and work (John 16:13);

and to represent believers before God as He prays for our needs with a heavenly language which we cannot speak nor understand (Rom. 8:26). His work is to make Jesus real to man.

1. *The Spirit in Relation to Sinners*

    * CONVINCES

    * CONVICTS

    * CONVERTS

(1) He *convinces* the sinner about the truth of Jesus Christ and presents Him as the object of faith. "But when the Comforter (Counselor, Helper, Advocate, Intercessor, Strenthener, Standby) Whom I will send to you from the Father, the Spirit of Truth . . . He (Himself) will testify regarding Me" (John 15:26). "He will honor and glorify Me (Christ)" (John 16:14).

(2) He *Convicts* the sinner of his sinfulness before God. "And when He comes, He will convict and convince the world and bring demonstration to it about sin and about righteousness—uprightness of heart and right standing with God—and about judgment: About sin, because they do not believe on Me—trust in, rely on and adhere to Me; About righteousness—uprightness of heart and right standing with God—because I go to My Father and you will see Me no longer; About judgment, because the ruler (prince) of this world (Satan) is judged and condemned and sentence already is passed upon him" (John 16:8–11).

Without this inner conviction, no sinner could ever come to know Christ. Jesus said, "No one is able to come to Me unless the Father Who sent Me attracts and draws him and gives him the desire to come to Me" (John 6:44).

The Christian witness must be constantly aware of and dependent upon the convicting work of the Spirit as he tries to lead men to Christ.

(3) He *Converts* the repentant sinner from death to life and gives him a new nature.

"But if any one does not possess the (Holy) Spirit of Christ, he is none of Him—he does not belong to Christ, (is not truly a child of God). But if Christ lives in you, (then although your natural) body is dead by reason of sin and guilt, the spirit is alive because of (the) righteousness (that He imputes to you)" (Rom. 8:9,10).

"He saved us, not because of any works of righteousness that we had done, but because of His own pity and mercy, by (the) cleansing (bath) of the new birth (regeneration) and renewing of the Holy Spirit" (Titus 3:5).

2. *The Holy Spirit in Relation to the Believer.*

* INDWELLS

* INFILLS

The Holy Spirit lives within the believer to form him to the image of Christ as he yields and surrenders to His guidance and control. Paul said, "My little children, for whom I am again suffering birth pangs until Christ is completely and permanently formed (molded) within you" (Gal. 4:19). It is not that we imitate Christ, but that He lives within us to be our life. "But if Christ lives in you, (then although your natural) body is dead by reason of sin and guilt, the spirit is alive because of (the) righteousness (that He imputes to you)" (Rom. 8:10).

(1) *The Spirit INDWELLS the Believer.*

"Do you not discern and understand . . . that God's Spirit has His permanent dwelling in you" (1 Cor. 3:16).

a. We have our salvation forever sealed by the Holy Spirit.

"And do not grieve the Holy Spirit of God, (do not offend, or vex, or sadden Him) by Whom you were sealed (marked, branded as God's own, secured) for the day of redemption—of final deliverance through Christ from evil and the consequences of sin" (Eph. 4:30).

b. We are given inner assurance that we are saved through the inner witness of the Spirit.

"The Spirit Himself (thus) testifies together with our own spirit, (assuring us) that we are children of God" (Rom. 8:16). (See also Gal. 4:6).

c. We have the Holy Spirit praying for our needs in a heavenly language we cannot use.

"The Spirit Himself goes to meet our supplication and pleads in our behalf with unspeakable yearnings and groanings too deep for utterance. And He Who searches the hearts of men knows what is in the mind of the (Holy) Spirit—what His intent is—because the Spirit intercedes and pleads (before God) in behalf of the saints according to and in harmony with God's will (Ps. 139:1,2)" (Rom. 8:26,27).

d. The Spirit strengthens the believer with inward power to face life's difficulties.

"May He grant you out of the rich treasury of His glory to be strengthened and reinforced with mighty power in the inner man by the (Holy) Spirit (Himself)—indwelling your innermost being and personality" (Eph. 3:16).

e. The Spirit guides the believer into the truth of God which gives light by which to live.

"Thy word is a lamp unto my feet, and a light unto my path" (Psa. 119:105). Only the Holy Spirit can turn on the light of truth. If He doesn't enlighten us, we will follow our own selfish ways (1 Cor. 2:14).

"He will guide you into all the truth . . ." (John 16:13). (See also John 14:26; 15:26; 1 Cor. 2:9–14; and 1 John 2:27)

f. The Spirit leads the believer in his daily walk in Christ.

"For if you live according to (the dictates of) the flesh you will surely die. But if through the power of the (Holy) Spirit you are habitually putting to death—make extinct, deaden—the (evil) deeds prompted by the body, you shall (really and genuinely) live forever. For all who are led by the Spirit of God are sons of God" (Rom. 8:13,14).

g. The Spirit inspires the believer in how to pray.

"So too the (Holy) Spirit comes to our aid and bears up in our weakness; for we do not know what prayer to offer nor how to offer it worthily as we ought" (Rom. 8:26). (See also Jude 20; Eph. 6:18.)

h. The Spirit produces Christlike characteristics in us as we yield to His control.

"But the fruit of the (Holy) Spirit, (the work which His presence within accomplishes)—is love, joy (gladness), peace, patience (an even temper, forbearance), kindness, goodness (benevolence), faithfulness;" "(Meekness, humility) gentleness, self-control (self-restraint, continence)" (Gal. 5:22, 23).

It is only as we allow the Holy Spirit to develop these characteristics within us that we have the ability to get along with one another (Col. 1:11).

i. The Spirit is grieved if we are not yielded to His control.

"And do not grieve the Holy Spirit of God" (Eph. 4:30).

"Do not quench (suppress or subdue) the (Holy) Spirit" (1 Thess. 5:19).

(2) The Holy Spirit *INFILLS* the yielding believer with power to do God's will in witnessing and service.

Every true believer has the Holy Spirit indwelling his life, but not every believer has the Spirit infilling his life with power for the work of God. It is not that the Spirit does not dwell fully within, but that He does not have complete control. Christ died that he might *purchase* us with His own blood, but he rose again and lives within us that he might *possess* us and be our Lord (Rom. 14:9).

The believer is to recognize that the Spirit is living fully within; that because of this he no longer has to be a slave to sin, but can know a life of victory (Rom. 8:10–13).

Now, the believer must daily surrender and yield his whole life to the Spirit's control, and He will infill him with power to do God's will in testimony and service. We receive the fulness of the Spirit the same as we received the new birth, BY FAITH!

"Then Jesus, full of and controlled by the Holy Spirit, returned from the Jordan, and was led in (by) the (Holy) Spirit for (during) forty days in the wilderness (desert) . . . Then Jesus went back full of and under the power of the (Holy) Spirit into Galilee" (Luke 4:1,14)

"(Just) as the Father has sent Me forth, so I am sending you. And having said this, He breathed on (them) and said to them, Receive (admit) the Holy Spirit" (John 20:21,22). How did God send forth His Son? In the power of the Spirit. This is how the Spirit desires to send us forth.

a. What is the purpose of the infilling of the Holy Spirit? The filling of the Spirit is not primarily intended to make believers happy, but to make them useful. The indwelling Spirit gives power to live joyfully and victoriously as we submit to His control; the infilling of the Spirit gives power to witness and work.

(a) The filling of the Spirit gives power to witness.

"But you shall receive power—ability, efficiency and might—when the Holy Spirit has come upon you; and you shall be My witnesses in Jerusalem and all Judea and Samaria and to the ends—the very bounds—of the earth" (Acts 1:8).

"And now, Lord, observe their threats and grant to Your bond servants (full freedom) to declare Your message fearlessly. And when they had prayed, the place in which they were assembled was shaken; and they were all filled with the Holy Spirit, and they continued to speak the Word of God with freedom and boldness and courage" (Acts 4:29,31).

(b) The filling of the Spirit gives power to work.

"How God anointed and consecrated Jesus of Nazareth with the (Holy) Spirit and with strength and ability and power; how He went about going good and in particular curing all that were harassed and oppressed by (the power of) the devil, for God was with Him" (Acts 10:38).

The gifts of service vary with the different areas of service to which God has called different persons. It is not for us to choose some place of service and then ask the Holy Spirit to qualify us for that task; it is not for us to select some gift and then ask the Holy Spirit to impart to us that gift. It is for us to simply put ourselves entirely at the disposal of the Holy Spirit to send us where He will, to select for us what kind of service He will, and to give what gift He will. Our position is that of unconditional surrender to Him. God will never lead us to any responsibility in which He will not give us the power to accomplish His will.

"Now there are distinctive varieties and distributions of endowments (extraordinary powers distinguishing certain Christians, due to the power of divine grace operating in their souls by the Holy Spirit) and that vary, but the (Holy) Spirit remains the same. To one is given in and through the (Holy) Spirit (the power to speak) a message of wisdom, and to another (the power to speak) a message of wisdom, and to another (the power to express) a word of knowledge and understanding according to the same (Holy) Spirit; To another (wonderworking) faith by the same (Holy) Spirit, to another the extraordinary powers of healing by the one Spirit; All these (achievements and abilities) are inspired and brought to pass by one and the same (Holy) Spirit, Who apportions to each person individually (exactly) as He chooses" (1 Cor. 12:4,8,9,11).

b. Who may receive infilling of the Holy Spirit?

The power for witnessing and working is given to every believer who is yielded to the Spirit's control.

A person may be born again by the Spirit and still not be empowered with the Spirit. In conversion there is an impartation of life, and the one who receives it is born again; in the anointing there is an impartation of power, and the one who is infilled or anointed is empowered for service.

With each opportunity of service there must be an empowering by the Spirit if our work is to please God. Peter was infilled on three different known occasions (Acts 2:4; Acts 4:8; Acts 4:31).

"And you shall receive the gift of the Holy Spirit. For the promise (of the Holy Spirit) is to and for you and your children, and to and for all that are far away, (even) to as many as the Lord and God invites and bids come to Himself (Isa. 57:19; Joel 2:32)" (Acts 2:38,39).

c. Why do we need the infilling of the Spirit to do God's work?

(a) Jesus Christ himself did not begin His earthly ministry until anointed with the Holy Ghost and power.

"How God anointed and consecrated Jesus of Nazareth with the (Holy) Spirit and with strength and ability and power; how He went about doing good and in particular curing all that were harassed and oppressed by (the power of) the devil, for God was with Him" (Acts 10:38).

(b) The disciples did not enter upon the work to which Christ called them until controlled by the Holy Spirit.

Even though the disciples had been with Jesus, and had been trained by Him, they were commanded not to begin until they had been endued with power from on high. The whole world was perishing, and they alone knew the saving truth; yet Jesus charged them to wait until empowered.

"You are witnesses of these things. And behold, I will send forth upon you What My Father has promised; but remain in the city (Jerusalem) until you are clothed with power from on high" (Luke 24:48,49).

(c) We, too, must be continuously controlled by the Spirit if we are to successfully do God's work.

If Jesus and the early disciples needed power from on high, what a testimony to the importance of our being anointed with the Holy Spirit for work that shall be acceptable to Christ! It is impossible to do the service that Christ expects without an empowerment from on high for each task. Supernatural work demands supernatural power.

d. How are we filled with the power of the Spirit?

(a) We must *realize* that the infilling of the Spirit is every believer's privilege before he does God's work.

"And you shall receive the gift of the Holy Spirit. For the promise (of the Holy Spirit) is to and for you and your children, and to and for all that are far away, (even) to as many as the Lord invites and bids come to Himself (Isa. 57:19; Joel 2:32)" (Acts 2:38,39).

(b) We must *confess* and *forsake* every sin, and make all wrongs right, then we may be cleansed.

"If we (freely) admit that we have sinned and confess our sins, He is faithful and just (true to His own nature and promises) and will forgive our sins (dismiss our lawlessness) and continuously cleanse us from all unrighteousness—everything not in conformity to His will in purpose, thought and action" (1 John 1:9).

"Remember that if your brother has any (grievance) against you, . . . go; first make peace with your brother" (Matt. 5:23,24).

"Do not ever let your wrath—your exasperation, your fury or indignation—last until the sun goes down" (Eph. 4:26).

"But if you do not forgive others their trespasses—their reckless and wilful sins, leaving them, letting them go and giving up resentment—neither will your Father forgive you your trespasses" (Matt. 6:15).

(c) We must *humble* ourselves, and die to self and self will, and yield completely to the control of the Spirit.

"Let this same attitude and purpose and (humble) mind be in you which was in Christ Jesus—Let Him be your example in humility— Who, although being essentially one with God and in the form of God (possessing the fullness of the attributes which make God God), did not think this equality with God was a thing to be eagerly grasped or retained; but stripped Himself (of all privileges and rightful dignity) so as to assume the guise of a servant (slave), in that He became like men and was born a human being:

"And after He had appeared in human form He abased and humbled Himself (still further) and carried His obedience to the extreme of death, even the death of the cross!

"Therefore (because He stooped so low), God has highly exalted Him and has freely bestowed on Him the name that is above every name; that in (at) the name of Jesus every knee should (must) bow, on heaven and on earth and under the earth, and every tongue (frankly and openly) confess and acknowledge that Jesus Christ is Lord, to the glory of God the Father.

"Therefore, my dear ones, as you have always obeyed . . . work out—cultivate, carry out to the goal and fully complete—your own salvation with reverence and awe and trembling. (Not in your own strength) for it is God Who is at work in you both to will and to work for His good pleasure and satisfaction and delight" (Phil. 2–5–13).

"The Holy Spirit is also, Whom God has bestowed on those who obey Him" (Acts 5:32).

In a sense Jesus was saying, "For to me to live is my Father." It is by this principle that we are to live a resurrected life. We must humble ourselves, die to self, and allow Christ to be that which is alive in us. Remember, Jesus said: "Let this mind (attitude) be in you." We must be able to say, "To me to live is Christ, to die is gain" (Phil. 1:21).

(d) We must *pray* and *ask* God by faith to infill us with power as we witness and work.

"And when they had prayed, the place in which they were assembled was shaken; and they were all filled with the Holy Spirit" (Acts 4:31). (See also Luke 11:13.)

If you do not have the enduement of power from the Holy Spirit upon your witness and work, it is because you have not claimed this privilege in Christ, or you have not fulfilled God's conditions of surrender and obedience.

"Be not drunk with wine, but be filled (addicted, controlled, intoxicated) with the Spirit" (Eph. 5:18).

APPENDIX

BIBLIOGRAPHY

ALLEN, MAVIS (EDITOR). *Bible Survey Series,* Nashville: Convention Press, 1969.

ANDERSON, R. A. *The Shepherd-Evangelist.* Washington: Review & Herald Publishers.

AUTREY, C. E. *Basic Evangelism.* Grand Rapids: Zondervan Publishing House, 1959.

————. *You Can Win Souls.* Nashville: Broadman Press.

ARCHIBALD, ARTHUR C. *Establishing the Convert.* Philadelphia: Judson Press, 1952.

BARCLAY, WILLIAM. *The Master's Men.* London: SCM Press, 1959.

————. *The Promise of the Spirit,* Philadelphia: The Westminster Press.

BIEDERWOLF, WILLIAM E. *Evangelism.* New York: Fleming J. Revell.

BISAGNO, JOHN R. *How to Build an Evangelistic Church.* Nashville: Broadman Press.

BONHOEFFER, DIETRICH. *The Cost of Discipleship.* New York: The Macmillan Co.

BRISCOE, STUART D. *The Fullness of Christ.* Grand Rapids: Zondervan Publishing House.

————. *Living Dangerously.* Zondervan Publishing House.

BRUCE, A. B. *The Training of the Twelve.* New York: Richard R. Smith Inc., 1930.

BRUCE, F. F. *Paul and His Converts.* Nashville: Abington Press.

BRIGHT, BILL. *Revolution Now.* San Bernardino: Campus Crusade for Christ, 1970.

CHAFIN, KENNETH L. *Help I'm A Layman.* Waco: Word Books.

COLEMAN, ROBERT E. *The Master Plan of Evangelism.* New York: Fleming H. Revell, 1970.

DOBBINS, GAINES S. *Evangelism According to Christ.* Nashville: Broadman Press.

————. *A Ministering Church.* Nashville: Broadman Press, 1960.

DRAKEFORD, JOHN W. *Counseling for Church Leaders.* Nashville: Broadman Press.

EDMAN, RAYMOND V. *They Found the Secret.* Grand Rapids: Zondervan Publishing House.

EDGE, FINDLEY B. *A Quest for Vitality in Religion.* Nashville: Broadman Press.

————. *Helping the Teacher.* Nashville: Broadman Press.

FISHER, FRED L. *Christiantiy Is Personal.* Nashville: Broadman Press.

HUNTER, JOHN. *Knowing God's Secrets.* Grand Rapids: Zondervan Publishing House.

————. *Let Us Go On to Maturity.* Zondervan Publishing House.

————. *Limiting God.* Zondervan Publishing House.

————. *Living the Christ Filled Life.* Zondervan Publishing House.

HALDEMAN, I. M. *How to Study the Bible.* Grand Rapids: Baker Book House.

LEAVELL, ROLAND Q. *Evangelism, Christ's Imperative Command.* Nashville: Broadman Press.

LAWRENCE. J. B. *The Holy Spirit in Evangelism.* Grand Rapids: Zondervan Publishing House.

MACARTNEY, CLARENCE E. *Great Interviews of Jesus.* Nashville: Abington Cokesbury Press.

McCALL, DUKE K. *What Is the Church?* Nashville: Broadman Press.

McDANIEL, GEORGE W. *The Churches of the New Testament.* Nashville: Broadman Press.

MOORE, WAYLAND B. *New Testament Follow-Up.* Grand Rapids: William B. Eerdmans.

NEE, WATCHMAN. *The Normal Christian Life.* Fort Washington, Pennsylvania: Christian Literature Crusade.

————. *Set, Walk, Stand.* Fort Washington: Christian Literature Crusade.

POWELL, SIDNEY W. *Fire on the Earth.* Nashville: Broadman Press.

————. *Where Are the Converts.* Nashville: Broadman Press.

RAVENHILL, LEONARD. *A Treasury of Prayer.* Minneapolis: Bethany Fellowship.

REES, PAUL. *Prayer and Life's Highest.* Grand Rapids: William B. Eerdmans.

SANNY, LORNE C. *Helping Others Find Christ.* Chicago: Moody Press.

SMITH, WILBURN M. *Profitable Bible Study.* Natick: W. A. Wilde Co.

————. *A Treasury of Books for Bible Study.* Natick: W. A. Wilde Co.

SWEENEY, GEORGE E. *Effective Evangelism.* New York: Harper & Brothers, 1953.

TAYLOR, JACK. *The Key to Triumphant Living.* Nashville: Broadman Press, 1971.

THOMAS, W. IAN. *The Saving Life of Christ.* Grand Rapids: Zondervan Publishing House.

————. *The Mystery of Godliness.* Grand Rapids: Zondervan Publishing House.

TRAINA, ROBERT A. *Methodical Bible Study.* New York: Biblical Seminary.

TROTMAY, DAWSON. *Born to Reproduce.* Lincoln: Back to the Bible Publishers, 1959.

TRUEBLOOD, ELTON. *The Company of the Committed.* New York: Harper & Brothers, 1961.

————. *Your Other Vacation.* New York: Harper & Brothers.

TRUMBULL, CHARLES G. *Victory in Christ.* Fort Washington, Pennsylvania: Christian Literature Crusade.

TURNER, CLYDE J. *The New Testament Doctrine of the Church.*
Nashville: Broadman Press.
UNKNOWN CHRISTIAN. *How to Live the Victorious Christian
Life.* Grand Rapids: Zondervan Publishing House.

MATERIALS

The author suggests the use of several specific items to implement his program of follow-up evangelism. (Note pages x–xi of the Author's Preface.)

1. *A Decision Card.* Printed decision cards are available from your book store, and book store personnel will be glad to help you make a choice. Baptist Book Stores carry a convenient church membership and decision form (with attached carbon), code number 4384–06.

2. *Sunday School Individual Record Card.* The author suggests that the basic Sunday School class attendance record card is all that is needed to keep check on the progress of the new member. Example: in Baptist Book Stores, code number 4388–05, individual record card.

3. *A Rubber Stamp for the Individual Record Card.* (Note page xi of the Author's Preface.) This is not available commercially, but it can be made up locally. The author's suggested wording:

NEW CHURCH MEMBER
Needs Special Care

4. *An Initial Visit Card.* This item is not available commercially and will need to be mimeographed or printed. (Note pp. x–xi of the Author's Preface, also p. 55.) For your convenience, a typical sample is reproduced full size herewith, pp. 126–127.

S.S. Worker_____

— TO BE FILLED OUT BY OFFICE —

INITIAL VISIT CARD

SUNDAY SCHOOL WORKER'S FOLLOW-UP REPORT
(Please try to make this visit within 48 hours)

New Member_____ Date_____

Address_____ Phone_____

Sunday School Dept._____ Class_____

Birthdate: Month_____ Day_____ Year_____

Decision: ☐ Salvation ☐ Transfer of Letter ☐ Rededication
          ☐ Special Service ☐ Other

— TO BE FILLED OUT BY SUNDAY SCHOOL WORKER —

DATE OF VISIT _____

Contacted by ☐ Visit *(Preferred)* ☐ Phone ☐ Letter
☐ I have encouraged New Member to complete the booklet, "Your Life in Christ"
☐ New Member has begun Lesson I.
☐ Have encouraged New Member to be faithful in Church Attendance
☐ Gave my testimony to New Member

Additional comments: _____
_____
_____

(Return this card to the Church Office)

(Front)

INITIAL VISIT CARD

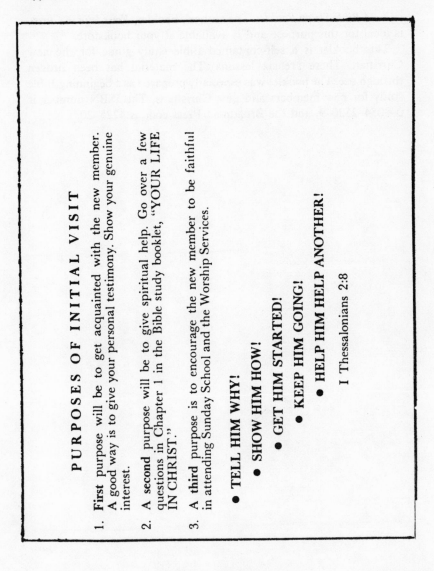

PURPOSES OF INITIAL VISIT

1. **First** purpose will be to get acquainted with the new member. A good way is to give your personal testimony. Show your genuine interest.

2. A **second** purpose will be to give spiritual help. Go over a few questions in Chapter 1 in the Bible study booklet, "YOUR LIFE IN CHRIST."

3. A **third** purpose is to encourage the new member to be faithful in attending Sunday School and the Worship Services.

- **TELL HIM WHY!**
  - **SHOW HIM HOW!**
    - **GET HIM STARTED!**
      - **KEEP HIM GOING!**
        - **HELP HIM HELP ANOTHER!**

        I Thessalonians 2:8

(Reverse Side)
INITIAL VISIT CARD

5. *A Bible Study Booklet.* The author's booklet, *Your Life in Christ,* is ideal for this purpose and is available at your bookstore.

This booklet is a self-contained Bible study guide for the new Christian. There are six lessons. The material has been proven through use. The booklet was especially prepared as a beginning Bible study for new members and new Christians. The ISBN number is 0–8054–2520–9, and the Broadman Press code is 4225–20.